The Old Burying Ground
THE HISTORY OF COLONIAL PARK CEMETERY

COLONIAL PARK.

THE
OLD BURYING GROUND:
COLONIAL PARK CEMETERY
SAVANNAH, GEORGIA
1750-1853

by
ELIZABETH CARPENTER PIECHOCINSKI

THE OGLETHORPE PRESS, INC.
Savannah, Georgia
1999

Publication of this book was assisted by a grant from the R. J. Taylor, Jr. Foundation. The Foundation is not responsible for content errors or omissions.

Elizabeth Carpenter Piechocinski
The Old Burying Ground: Colonial Park Cemetery, Savannah, Georgia, 1750-1853

ISBN(hardcover) 1-891495-08-9
    (paperback) 1-891495-09-7

1. Genealogy, Savannah GA, 18th and 19th century. 2. History, Georgia, 18th and 19th century. 3. Social conditions. 4. Medical practices, diseases. 5. Burial practices. 6. Gravestone symbolism.

Library of Congress Catalog Card Number 99-75959

Cover design by J. M. Connan
Cover photo is courtesy of Georgia Historical Society, Savannah, Georgia

DEDICATION

This book is lovingly dedicated to John,
my husband, who first introduced me to
Colonial Park Cemetery thirty-some years ago.

TABLE OF CONTENTS

INTRODUCTION

Cemeteries have always intrigued people. By their very nature, they invoke a sense of sadness, mystery, immortality, and even apprehension. It is difficult to pass by a cemetery and not be touched by some emotion, however brief.

Old country graveyards, early burial grounds, and the urban cities of the dead tend to hold an appeal that is not always easy to define. Perhaps it is the folk art that captures one's attention; or the flowery epitaphs of a long ago time; or the elaborate sculpture; or the history that surrounds notable figures. Whatever the individual appeal, this book will attempt in some small way to guide the reader through an early American cemetery that reflects the history of a southern city where the past is a constant companion to the present.

Colonial Park Cemetery, opened in 1750, was the second public burial ground in the new colony of Georgia. In use for one hundred and three years, it was the resting place for the early settlers in the colony.

Over the course of its history, it has been the victim of weather, politics, war, vandalism, neglect, and well-meaning, but misguided, attempts to maintain it. Out of nearly 10,000 burials, only approximately 600 stones and monuments remain. Its history has been prey to the ravages of time, its inhabitants fading into the dim past. Yet this old burial ground contains the remains of the ancestors of modern-day Georgians, and many New England families have connections here as well. This is an attempt to rescue these names from oblivion and make them available to those who seek to trace their family histories, as well as to guide the casual visitor through the site.

The information on which this book is based was gathered from a number of various sources which include old city records, early newspaper accounts, and other printed publications, including *Some Early Epitaphs in Georgia,* which was published by the Colonial Dames in Georgia in 1924.

Most information was compared with an on-site visual inspection of the gravestones in order to insure correct information, and also to insure that none was overlooked. Where discrepancies occurred in the various sources, I chose the information that seemed to the be most reasonable and logical, according to available data. I avoided including statements or information that could not be documented in some way. A bibliography listing the sources for this material is to be found at the back of this book.

The Old Burying Ground
THE HISTORY OF COLONIAL PARK CEMETERY

The Old Burying Ground
THE HISTORY OF COLONIAL PARK CEMETERY

The first public burial ground in Savannah was included in James Oglethorpe's plan for Savannah in 1733. It was located in Percival Ward, Holland Tything, Lots 2 and 3 — in the area bordered by York, Bull, Oglethorpe, and Whitaker streets. This burial ground was used only about seventeen years. It was closed to interments in 1750 when the city established a new burial ground. The original burial ground was abandoned, and eventually all traces of it disappeared as the quickly expanding city consigned it to oblivion. Today, only a plaque notes its location on York Street.

The new burial ground, established in 1750, was located outside the city walls on the southeast portion of the city. A 1780 map shows this burial ground was enclosed, with a gate on the east side. Christ Episcopal Church, the first church in Savannah, acquired the ownership of the burial ground in 1758. It was operated and maintained as a public burial ground by Christ Church for the next ninety-eight years. The burying ground was enlarged by the Act of 1763, extending its area "to the line of Abercorn Street" on the west, and 100 feet to the south.

Soon after the British abandoned Savannah to the Americans in 1782, the old British earthworks were destroyed, and the burying ground was incorporated into the city grid. A city ordinance of 1789 stated that the Christ Church Burying Ground, by this time 210 feet in width and 380 feet in length, was too small for its intended purpose. A county surveyor was authorized to measure and lay off 120 feet eastward and 290 feet southward in order to enlarge the cemetery to a total of 500 square feet. This addition was to be a "public burial ground for the interment of all Christian people of whatever denomination ... and not to be considered as belonging to ... the Episcopal Church of Savannah, commonly called Christ Church."

Vandalism is not a problem unique to modern times. In 1783, contributions were solicited to rebuild the wall around the cemetery which had been damaged by the British during their occupation of Savannah. Citizens complained that corpses were being dug up by dogs and wild animals and emphasized the need for a fence to enclose the cemetery. Theatrical events were staged to raise funds for the wall, and there are indications that George Washington, on his visit to Savannah in 1791, may have contributed to this fund.

The resulting brick wall, containing 300,000 bricks, was built in 1791 and was to stand for the next one hundred years. A new gate was placed at the intersection of South Broad and Lincoln streets. In 1813, the Chatham Academy was constructed, and, in 1818, additional city lots were laid out west of the burying ground.

The only paved pathway ran from the main entrance at South Broad Street to the exit at Perry Lane. This was a brick walk, and was used exclusively by horse-drawn hearses. The city bought a horse-drawn hearse in 1803, and the burials were in the old South Broad Street burying ground. In October 1803, an ordinance was passed which required that a burial register be kept by the Board of Health. Prior to this time, records of deaths and burials were kept by the churches in the city.

In 1812, a second gate was created at the north end of the west wall. A stranger's or foreigners' burial ground for newcomers or non-residents was also provided outside the wall along the east side of the property to accommodate the rising death rate due to the yellow fever epidemics which swept through the city periodically. In 1819, the aldermen directed that the sexton was "to appear in a black dress of decent appearance and fit for the solemnity of the burial service." By 1846, plantings of trees and shrubs were provided "to protect citizens from "poisonous effluvia" arising from the site, and believed to be the cause of yellow fever. Earlier maps show a double row of trees around the perimeter.

In 1849, the city government was petitioned by the citizens to establish a new modern burial ground outside the city walls. Accordingly, the city allotted one hundred acres of the newly purchased Springfield Plantation for the purpose of a public burial ground to be named Laurel Grove. The first sale of lots there took place in 1852.

County health officials invited all citizens who had relatives buried in the South Broad Street Cemetery to remove and re-inter their family remains in the new cemetery, free of charge. During the period from November 1852 to April 1888, as many as six hundred burials were removed from the Old or Brick Cemetery, as it was called, to Laurel Grove. The Evergreen-Bonaventure Cemetery opened to public burial after 1849, and Catholic Cemetery opened in 1853, and another one hundred sixty remains were relocated to these cemeteries, especially to Catholic Cemetery.

On July 1, 1853, South Broad Street Cemetery, which had reached its capacity, was officially closed to interments. A few later burials did occur, but they were exceptions, the most notable of which was the relocation and interment of the remains of Samuel Elbert and his wife from Rae's Hall to Colonial Cemetery in 1924. No longer in active use, the Old Cemetery became prey to neglect and vandalism.

When Union troops entered Savannah in December of 1864, they used the walled cemetery to quarter horses and assemble wagons. The soldiers caused further damage to stones and vaults, some of which is still visible today. Some stones were defaced, while others were removed from their original locations. Further deterioration and neglect after the Civil War continued.

In 1868, the Old Cemetery Association was formed to attempt the first preservation of the site. Private and public funds were used to repair the damaged brick wall, and also the gates which had been nailed shut in 1865. Lack of continued support prevented any further preservation efforts by the group.

The next attempt at preserving the site came in 1887 when the Georgia Historical Society attempted to record the markers and epi-taphs. Over seven hundred epitaphs were gathered, and a pen-and-ink sketch of the cemetery was made which showed the location of some of the graves.

Because of the neglect and poor condition of the site, and because of the concern of the citizens, the city made an attempt to purchase the property from Christ Church. This effort ended in a lawsuit between the church and the city which was resolved in favor of the city in 1895. This lawsuit reflected the concern by Christ Church that the city would develop this valuable piece of property, remove the walls, cut streets, and generally desecrate the site as had been done with the first burial ground.

The case was eventually settled, allowing the city to purchase the site, with restricting covenants preventing the cutting of new streets through the cemetery, and stating that the city must forever preserve the site as a final resting place of the dead. The city did get the right to tear down the walls, but the stipulation was given that the property was to be used "as a public park to be called Colonial Park". If the mentioned covenants were violated, the property would revert to Christ Church. This restriction was invoked in 1922 to prevent the city from extending Lincoln Street through the cemetery.

The old South Broad Street cemetery became a public park in 1896, under the jurisdiction of the Park and Tree Commission. A beautification program was begun that year which included the laying of pathways, installation of benches and trash receptacles, and landscaping. Some restoration of tombs and stones was also done. Unfortunately, a number of stones were pulled up during this beautification program to make room for new walkways. This is evident in the before and after photographs taken in 1896 and again in 1897 when the beautification project was completed. Those stones, along with other misplaced stones whose original locations were unknown, were mounted on the east wall to preserve them.

In 1913, the Daughters of the American Revolution erected the archway at the northwest corner of the cemetery to honor the American patriots interred there. This entrance at the corner of Abercorn and Oglethorpe Avenue is now the main entrance to the cemetery. An attempt was made by the city in 1922 to open Lincoln Street from Perry Lane to Oglethorpe Avenue, but the original covenant with Christ Church prevented this proposal from occurring. The Colonial Dames of Georgia transcribed all of the epitaphs in the cemetery in 1924, and published their work in *Some Early Epitaphs in Georgia*, an endeavor which has proved to be an invaluable source in locating and identifying deteriorated markers.

Vandalism continued throughout ensuing years, and the city erected a wrought iron railing around three sides of the cemetery in 1956. The old east wall was left in place. More restoration efforts were undertaken. Stones were cleaned, and, in some cases, reset; additional landscaping work was done; historical markers were placed near the most historically significant grave sites. Another preservation effort is currently underway by the Savannah Park and Tree Commission.

In August of 1998, a team of archaeologists from Chicora Foundation, Incorporated, a public, non-profit archaeological and historical research organization based in Columbia, South Carolina, used a penetrometer to locate probable grave sites. The penetrometer measures soil compaction and thus identifies areas where the soil has been disturbed. The purpose of this exploration is to identify grave sites so that they may be placed on a base map which will show the location of all of the graves and other features of Colonial Cemetery As of this writing, the locations of more than eight thousand unmarked graves have been identified.

From more recent evaluations of the site, no evidence of mass graves from the yellow fever epidemics have been located. Mass graves would likely have been used for strangers dying in Savannah, and thus, would more likely be located in the Strangers' Burial Ground which was once where the Police Barracks parking lot is today.

CULTURAL DIVERSITY
IN COLONIAL CEMETERY

A visitor to Colonial Cemetery soon discovers that a very diverse group of individuals lies interred here. This should not be surprising when it is recalled that this was to be a final resting place for all people, regardless of religious persuasion. While this diversity is scattered throughout the cemetery, there are certain concentrations of burials that appear rather quickly.

The southwest section of the cemetery which borders Abercorn Street contains a large number of Catholic burials beginning roughly with the brick vault of Father LeMoine and extending toward Perry Lane. There are a number of grave sites of early French refugees from the French Revolution in France and from the revolution in Saint Domingue or Haiti. A few of these stones have French inscriptions, with little or no English. There are also a large number of Irish Catholics buried in this section. With few exceptions, all of the Catholic burials here are marked with a cross on the stone. The majority give detailed information about the birthplace of these people, including not only the village or city, but also the county, and sometimes the parish. A few stones have Latin inscriptions.

While the brick wall on the east side of the cemetery contains mostly stones of people of English extraction, there are still a number of Irish stones as well, and even a couple of Italian and Portuguese burials.

Scattered throughout the cemetery are the graves of New Englanders who arrived in Savannah in the early 1800's. Their influence is seen in some of the older stones. Their stones frequently give their place of birth or origin, and sometimes the reason for their being in Savannah.

Many came South for health reasons. It is on these stones that one often encounters illnesses such as consumption, which many believed would improve in the warmer southern climate. A few of these stones also give the person's educational background.

A number of Scottish people, mostly males, are also to be found, again listing their origins. At least one of these has thistles carved on the stone. Quite a few have emblems of freemasonry as well. One of the Scottish stones contains a biography of the young man's short life, including the fact that he inherited a Glasgow brewery. His brother was the author of that epitaph. Perhaps the two most famous Scots to be buried in Colonial Cemetery were Colonel John Maitland and General Lachlan McIntosh.

There are also burials of many Irish, as well as Jews, Welsh, Spanish, Moravians, Germans, Swiss, and Salzburgers to be found throughout the cemetery. These were all part of the fabric of life in colonial Savannah.

MORTALITY RATES AND EPIDEMICS

As one strolls through Colonial Cemetery, or any very old cemetery, for that matter, he is struck by the large number of women and children interred there. In the eighteenth and nineteenth centuries, mortality rates were extremely high. This was due in large measure to the poor sanitary conditions and also to the lack of adequate medical attention.

During this period one of the leading causes of death among women was childbirth. Large families were the desired norm, and women married at a rather young age. It is not uncommon to find women bearing children at the rate of one every year and a half. Many infants did not survive the first two years of their lives. Stillbirths were common. Women often died in childbirth due to poor medical care and lack of antiseptic conditions. Infants and children were subject to a variety of ailments and diseases, and were too frequently the first victims of the numerous epidemics that plagued the colony. In reading early mortuary records, childbed fever (puerperal fever), and infantile disease are commonly listed causes of death. Smallpox, scarlet fever, measles, worms, and convulsions or spasms are other frequently mentioned causes of death among children.

Medical treatment often included bleeding, the use of leeches, purges, herbs, and many other procedures that seem rather barbaric today in light of modern medicine. Often the doctor or midwife relied on various folk medicines, experience, and even experimentation to treat complaints and diseases.

Aside from those mentioned above, other common causes of death were mortification (gangrene), drowning, delirium tremens, brain fever (encephalitis), consumption (tuberculosis), inflammation of the bowels (appendicitis), lock jaw, and various fevers. Insanity was sometimes listed as a cause of death as well.

In reading some of the old death registers and newspaper

accounts, the cause of an individual's death was often described in great detail, outlining the incidents that led to the person's demise. Some seem a little strange, such as the case of a Mrs. Cox who died in 1765 on a plantation a few miles from Savannah. According to her obituary, she entered one of the outhouses with some lighted sticks in her hand. Unfortunately that particular outhouse was used to store a keg of gunpowder which ignited from a spark, blowing up part of the house and severely burning Mrs. Cox, who died the next day. Humorous as this incident may appear, one must remember that on a farm or plantation, the term "outhouse" at that period of time was more likely to refer to a storage building than to a privy or "necessary" as they were sometimes called.

Other accounts evoke a sense of outrage as they recall overt acts of cruelty, as in the case of James and William Bayley, the fourteen and sixteen year-old boys whose stepmother refused to let James come into the house, and he died of exposure to intense cold in January of 1808. His brother William died the next day as a result of having to eat dirt. Their father was out of town and returned just before James died.

Some of the deaths were attributed to suicide. Life was undeniably hard in the early days of the colony, and, as is certainly true today, some had great difficulty adjusting to the demands of eighteenth century living. In January of 1786, Captain John Darthiague stunned his friends and acquaintances by shooting himself in the head with not one, but two, pistols. He lingered for nearly ten days before dying. An inquest rendered the verdict of " Insanity, at the time he committed the act." He was "decently interred" in the city burial ground.

Throughout my research I encountered a large number of deaths attributed to drowning. A huge portion of the population did not know how to swim. Yet, there are numerous accounts of people falling off wharves, falling from ships, overturning boats and canoes, bathing in the river, and attempting to cross rivers. Few of them were rescued in time.

Prevailing medical practices of the day, such as bleeding a patient for a variety of complaints and illnesses, also contributed to a large number of deaths. Other deaths were caused by the use of home remedies, some of which were detrimental, and of course, the lack of knowledge of proper sanitary and antiseptic practices. In an interesting sidelight to medical practices of the period, in 1805 the county health officer issued a notice urging smallpox vaccinations for any persons who had not had either smallpox or "kine" pox. Since the first vaccination of a human occurred in England in 1796, the health officers in Savannah were not slow in adopting the vaccine. Inoculations for smallpox became compulsory in 1816 in Savannah.

The health of the citizens in Savannah in 1807 was generally very poor. A special committee on health concluded that burial places in or near a city contributed to poor health. Accordingly, trees were planted around the wall of the cemetery to "imbibe the impurities" from the atmosphere. This idea was again suggested in 1843.

Since the months of August, September, and October seemed to be the sickliest months in the city, the City Council took steps to alleviate some of the sickness by proposals which they felt would be beneficial. They recommended to the military commandant and other military officers that the custom of firing guns and playing music at funerals be discontinued during the previously mentioned months. It was believed that such practices were exceedingly harmful to those who were sick. This was later expanded to include drumbeats and firing salutes before 10:00 a.m. on the occasion of the marriage of a militia member.

While yellow fever and other diseases were always prevalent in the low country, there were periodic outbreaks of epidemic proportions. The major epidemics that had the greatest impact on Savannah are listed below:

1820—First yellow fever epidemic
1854—Second yellow fever epidemic
1876—Third yellow fever epidemic

YELLOW FEVER

Yellow fever differed from the other fevers that occurred on a fairly regular basis in the low country. In addition to the usual chills and fever associated with malaria and the other seasonal fevers that were common in the late summer and early autumn, it attacked quickly, producing severe back pains, painful suppression of urine, and jaundice. These symptoms were followed by uncontrollable hemorrhaging of the gums, nose and stomach. The terminal symptoms were the "black vomit," convulsions, delirium, and coma. The lapse into a deep coma prompted one Savannah doctor to comment that it was likely that many patients who contracted yellow fever were buried alive.

Medical men had postulated a number of theories regarding the nature of the disease, but the general opinion seemed to attribute yellow fever to the seasonal irregular behavior of the blood. Like many of the other fevers which seemed to originate in the marshes and lowlands, yellow fever seemed to be most prevalent during July, August, September, and October. As cooler weather arrived and the first frosts occurred, the disease tended to disappear.

A fire in January of 1820 had caused massive destruction of property in Savannah. Much of the city lay in ruin. Added to that devastation were torrential spring rains which produce conditions favorable to the ever-present mosquito population. In August of that same year, a ship arriving in port from the West Indies brought with it the dreaded yellow fever. In the ensuing epidemic, spread by the female *Aedes aegypti* mosquito which found a friendly environment in the surrounding area of rice plantations and marshes, Savannah lost nearly seven hundred citizens in a three-month period.

That the loss was not even greater was no doubt due, in some measure, to the fact that many people had left Savannah because

The stone of Joseph Fox, a victim of the 1820 yellow fever epidemic.

The stone of Dr. James W. Cotton, one of the victims of the 1820 yellow fever epidemic.

Isaac Robins and his year-old daughter, Sarah. They died within a day of each other, two more victims during the 1820 epidemic.

their property had been destroyed by fire, and they were temporarily living with relatives elsewhere. Others routinely sent their families inland during the hot summer months to escape both the heat and the fevers that proliferated during those months. Thus, only about fifteen hundred people remained in the city when the major outbreak occurred. The doctors and the clergy felt it was their duty to provide care and comfort to those remaining in the city. While struggling to provide medical care for those stricken with the fever, at least ten physicians and three medical students contracted the fever themselves and died.

Of the known six hundred and sixty-six victims, only some forty stones mark the graves of yellow fever victims who died between June and November of 1820. With as many as ten or more deaths per day, it was impossible to conduct that many funerals. According to one newspaper account, nineteen persons died in one day. It was said that nineteen out of every twenty persons who contracted the disease died. There was little else the population could do except utilize mass burial procedures. Today, an historic marker pays mute tribute to those stricken by the fever in 1820.

Two later epidemics followed the one in 1820. In 1854, more than one thousand of Savannah's citizens died. By the time of the 1876 epidemic, changes were taking place in the city regarding sanitation practices and public health policies, and stringent quarantine policies were instituted which effectively put an end to future epidemics in Savannah.

1820 YELLOW FEVER VICTIMS
WHOSE GRAVES ARE KNOWN

NAME	DATE OF DEATH	AGE	OCCUPATION
1. John Newton	June 11		
2. Richard Riley	June 13	29	Laborer
3. Jeremiah Castoff	June 29	23	Ship's Mate
4. Christopher Riley	July 6	32	Laborer
5. Patrick Stanton	July 16	32	Merchant
6. Daniel Sake	July 18	30	Carpenter
7. David Pendergast	July 21	24	Shopkeeper
8. Ann Charlton	Aug. 2	26	
9. Honora Lawlor	Aug. 4	32	
10. Miles Jones	Aug. 8	33	
11. Mary M. Orme	Aug. 18	20	

12. Frederick Ball	Aug. 18		
13. William Woodbridge	Aug. 22	40	Merchant
14. John C. Gibson	Aug. 28	35	
15. Elizabeth Kirkling	Aug. 29	7	
16. Sarah Ann Robins	Sept. 41		
17. John McCarty	Sept. 13	2	
18. T. E. Lloyd	Sept. 14	33	Lawyer
19. Bridget Gillespie	Sept. 14	16	
20. Joseph Fox	Sept. 17	23	Teacher
21. Martha Deloney	Sept. 19	55	
22. Elias Ross	Sept. 19	27	Bricklayer
23. R. M. Berrien	Sept. 20	25	Physician
24. Jane Elon	Sept. 20	19	
25. Frances Ingold Gladhill	Sept. 23	30	
26. Augusta M. Merriam	Sept. 23	26	Governess
27. James W. Cotton	Sept. 27	23	Physician
28. Amos Dow	Sept. 27	28	
29. George Parker	Sept. 28		
30. Joseph Muir	Oct. 1	40	Merchant
31. J. W. Gladhill	Oct. 2	5	
32. Jacob Smith	Oct. 3	40	Carpenter
33. Michael Leahy	Oct. 5	25	Bricklayer
34. Benjamin Tutell	Oct. 12	26	Carpenter
35. Maria Thompson	Oct. 13	18	Milliner
36. Joseph Tatem	Oct. 14	24	Apothecary
37. John G. Gibson	Oct. 16		
38. Elizabeth O. Pettigrew	Oct. 17	26	
39. Charles H. Morel	Oct. 19	22	Clerk
40. Louis Muir	Oct. 19	13	
41. Charles H. Patterson	Oct. 29	29	Carpenter
42. Sarah Johnston	Nov. 3	44	
43. Ann Drysdale	Nov. 3	52	
44. Elizabeth Boynton	Nov. 3	30	
45. Peter Neville	Nov. 30	30	
46. Robert Fair	Dec. 18	45	Shoemaker

THE FAMILY VAULTS

U pon entering Colonial Park Cemetery, one of the first things to catch the visitor's eye is the brick family vault. These rather strange looking structures are a feature of the cemetery that invites all sorts of speculation as to their purpose and construction.

According to one of the archaeologists with the Chicora Foundation, burial vaults of this type seem to be unique to the Savannah and Charleston areas. There are three such brick vaults located in Sandersville, Georgia. They are not common along the eastern seaboard. Today about fifty of these old brick family vaults remain in Colonial Park. Originally there were many more than this number.

Contrary to first impressions, these are not above ground burials. The major portion of these vaults is situated below ground, perhaps as far as four to six feet. They were constructed much like a below ground cellar or basement, with brick walls and a floor paved with either brick or some other material. Usually three tiers of shelves are found along three sides. A short flight of steps leads from ground level down into the vault. Three tiers of shelves are arranged along three sides of the walls, each tier being separated from the next by approximately eighteen to twenty inches, just enough to allow a coffin or, in some cases, a shrouded corpse to be placed on a shelf. A large burial urn was sometimes placed in the center of the floor. When the vault became crowded and more space was needed, the older burials which had disintegrated to mere bones were placed in the urn, thereby freeing shelf space for additional burials. As this practice was repeated, the bones of family members eventually mingled in the central urn, thus reinforcing the idea of the family together in death.

The part of the vault that is visible on the surface is actually the roof of the subterranean room. Decorative brickwork forms either end, one of which holds the doorway. The archway at ground level which is often visible is actually the top arch of the door. The brick used in the construction of the tomb was usually a fine quality brick, while that used to seal the entrance was less expensive since it would be removed when necessary to permit new burials.

During the Federal occupation of Savannah in 1864, many of the vaults were opened by Union soldiers seeking loot reportedly hidden there, or to form shelter from the cold. There were reports by people living in Savannah during that period stating that many of the graves were desecrated by soldiers who even went so far as to pulling corpses from the tombs in search of jewelry and other valuables, and scattering bones on the ground outside.

One account mentions that some of the soldiers had rigged stovepipes in the vaults so that they could build fires inside the vaults to keep warm. It was also during this time that the soldiers amused themselves by carving graffiti on the stones, and also changing dates and ages on some of the stones. Children in later years used the vaults to play in, until their mothers put a stop to the practice for fear they would contract some disease from the tombs.

Aside from the usual gravestones, there are also single crypts and single vaults, as well as table tombs. One of the more unusual vaults is that of Thomas Purse and Daniel Gugel. This very large square stone slides to one side to allow entrance to that particular family tomb. Still others consist of a brick-lined box set in the earth with a slab covering the top. The large slabs that are now flush with the ground were originally raised on brick pillars or box-like enclosures. When other cemeteries in the city opened, many of the monuments and vaults were dismantled and erected in both Laurel Grove and in Bonaventure cemeteries.

Two different types of table tombs in Colonial Cemetery.

IDENTIFIED FAMILY VAULTS

1. Gugel-Purse Vault
2. Scarbrough Vault
3. McIntosh Vault (no longer in existence)
4. LeMoine (?) Vault
5. Waldron-Snider Vault-1838
6. Habersham Vault
7. Andrew McIntire Vault
8. George Wallace Hunter Vault
9. James Hunter Vault—1839
10. Owen Foley Vault—1849
11. Richard Wylly Vault
12. Graham-Mossman Vault
13. Noble Jones Vault
14. Tiot Vault
15. Claghorn Vault
16. Tufts Vault
17. Screven Vault
18. Benjamin Burroughs Vault

19. Davies Vault
20. Shellman Vault
21. Santini Vault
22. Thomasson Vault
23. Tebeau Vault
24. Schick Vault
25. Brigham Vault
26. George Oliver Vault
27. Hulse Vault
28. White Vault
29. Johnston Vault
30. Christie Vault
31. Lamb Vault
32. Thompson Vault

HISTORIC BURIALS

JAMES HABERSHAM VAULT

The Habersham vault has a very large white marble tablet inserted in its front. The tablet has a large relief carving of a crown and a cross. This vault contains the remains of James Habersham who was born in Yorkshire, England, in 1712. Little is known about Habersham's early life, but he came to Savannah in 1734, along with his good friend, George Whitefield.

Habersham began his life in the royal colony of Georgia as a schoolmaster at Bethesda, the orphanage of which he was one of the founders, along with George Whitefield. He married Mary Bolton, one of the older orphans at Bethesda, and had three sons: Joseph, John, and James. He entered into business with Francis Harris to become the first merchants engaged in exporting and importing goods. In 1754, Sir James Habersham became secretary of the province, and in 1767, he was appointed president of the assembly when Governor James Wright took a leave of absence.

When war between the colonies and England became imminent, Habersham was dismayed to find that his sons all declared their sympathies with the colonies. It was his son, Major Joseph Habersham, who became one of the "Liberty Boys," and, in a bold move, walked past sentinels in Governor Wright's own home where the royal council was meeting, placed his hand on Wright's shoulder, and said, "Sir James, you are my prisoner!" Thus, Major Habersham went down in history as the man who arrested the royal governor.

The royal governor eventually escaped his house arrest, and made his way to the warship *Scarborough* which transported him to safety in England. Sir James Habersham was appointed as president of the royal council to replace Wright.

The Honorable James Habersham, who had traveled to the

North for health reasons, died in Brunswick, New Jersey, in the summer of 1775.

Habersham's son, Major James Habersham, died in 1799, at the age of fifty-four. His brother, Major John Habersham, who had attained his rank in the First Continental Regiment of Georgia, later served in Congress, and had become Collector of the Port in Savannah, died in 1799, at the age of forty-five. Also interred in this vault is Mary Bolton Habersham who died in 1763.

THE GRAHAM-MOSSMAN VAULT

The Graham-Mossman vault is the second in a row of four vaults, perpendicular to Oglethorpe Avenue. This vault has had an interesting history, beginning in 1779, and continuing up to to 1981.

The vault was built as a family vault for Lt. Governor John Graham, a loyal British subject, who also owned a plantation, Mulberry Grove, on the west side of the city. The vault had never been used until October 25, 1779, when Lt. Col. John Maitland, 71st Scots Regiment of the British army, died of malaria shortly after the Siege of Savannah, in which he played a major role in the capture of Savannah by British forces. *The Royal Gazette* reported his death and his subsequent burial in the Graham vault.

In 1785, the American government awarded the confiscated Mulberry Grove Plantation to one of its Revolutionary heroes, Major-General Nathanael Greene, in recognition of his service to the country. Presumably, Graham's confiscated property also included the family vault at the Old Burying Ground. This claim would be challenged in later years by some of Graham's descendants.

On the 19th of June, 1786, Nathanael Greene died at Mulberry Plantation of what was said to be a heat stroke. His body was brought into the city by boat and taken to a friend's house, that of Nat Pendleton, on Yamacraw Bluff, near what is now Bay and Barnard streets. At five o'clock that afternoon, Greene's body was escorted to the old cemetery by the Chatham Artillery and placed in the Graham vault.

On April 4, 1790, the vault was once again opened to receive the remains of Greene's son, George Washington Greene, who drowned near Mulberry Grove when his canoe overturned in the river.

By 1819, the burial place of Nathanael Greene had been forgotten. A committee appointed by the city government of Savannah tried unsuccessfully to locate Greene's burial site. The city did erect a tall monument in Johnson Square in 1829, commemorating Greene's service in the American Revolution.

In the years that followed, James Mossman, a relative of John Graham, and his wife Elizabeth Mossman, had returned to Savannah, and had put forth claims that the confiscated property of John Graham did not include the family vault. Two stories circulated during the ensuing years regarding the burial of Greene.

One was that Mrs. Mossman had her Negro slaves remove Greene's remains from the vault at night and had them thrown into a creek.

The Habersham family vault.
Photo by Stacey Yongue

The Graham-Mossman vault where once rested the remains of General Nathanael Greene, his son George Washington Greene, and also Colonel John Maitland.

The other version stated that she had Greene's remains removed and buried at night in an unmarked grave elsewhere in the cemetery.

Neither of these stories had any basis in fact. There were no Graham remains in the vault at the time of Greene's death. This was a new vault that only been utilized once, for the burial of John Maitland, prior to the interment of Greene.

Mrs. Mossman died in 1802, and her husband, James, died in 1803. There was no record of a funeral or a burial of either of them, and it is likely that one or both of them died of yellow fever and were buried in a common grave, as was the practice for victims of fevers or contagious diseases. Elizabeth Mossman's obituary is evidence that her upstanding character would not have permitted her to indulge in such acts as the stories indicated.

The Graham vault was opened once again in 1845 to permit the burial of Robert Scott, a relative by marriage of the Mossman's. Mrs. Greene had remarried and moved away from Savannah, and the Mossmans had apparently reclaimed the vault. However, with the exception of Robert Scott, no other family members or relatives of the Mossmans were interred in the vault.

When Union forces entered Savannah in December of 1864, the soldiers quartered horses and heavy equipment in the old cemetery. The soldiers broke open a number of vaults, searching for loot, or to use as shelter. Vandalism was common as the soldiers desecrated grave sites. The identifying stone plaques placed on the vaults were destroyed or removed. As a result, no one could later remember who owned which vaults.

In 1901, Asa Bird, president of the Rhode Island Society of the Cincinnati, came to Savannah with the express purpose of locating the grave of Nathanael Greene. On March 1st of that year the mayor of Savannah gave the city permission to open four vaults in order to determine which, if any, held Greene's remains. This was necessary because the identifying stones had been removed or destroyed during the Union occupation of Savannah in 1864.

The first vault was opened, and was soon determined to be that of the Wylly family. The next vault was passed over because it was believed to be the Noble Jones vault, and it was known that the Jones family had removed the remains of that vault to Bonaventure Cemetery and thus, was empty. When the next vault was entered, it was found to be empty, indicating that it, not the second, belonged to the Jones family. The last vault in the row proved to be the Tiot vault.

When the committee opened the previously skipped second vault, the remains of several burials were apparent. Investigation of the left side of the vault uncovered the remains of two persons with evidence that established them as belonging to General Greene and also his son, George Washington Greene. The right side of the vault contained a coffin in reasonably good condition. A coffin plate identified this burial as that of Robert Scott, who died in 1845.

The remains of Greene and his son were removed. These were placed in the monument on Johnson Square with appropriate ceremony in 1902. Scott's remains were left undisturbed, and the vault was sealed.

The story of the Graham vault was not over, however. Its first occupant, John Maitland, would be the impetus for yet another opening of the vault.

John Maitland was born in 1732 in Laude, Scotland. His family castle of Thirlestone was a brief refuge for Bonnie Prince Charlie after the Battle of Culloden Moor in 1745. Maitland was then fourteen years old.

In 1758, John Maitland, then in service in the British Army, lost his right arm in a military engagement in Spain against the French. He was the only commissioned officer to be wounded in that encounter. He later became a member of the House of Commons in England, and when war broke out with the colonies in America, he led his 71st Highlander troops over to aid the British forces. As a military leader, he won the respect and admiration of both sides, and had his troops adopt a red feather to wear in their bonnets so that his foe, General Washington, would know whom to credit for their accomplishments in battle. This identifying badge of honor is still used today by the Black Watch Regiment.

At the siege of Savannah in 1779, it was Maitland and his Highlanders who slipped into Savannah from his post at Beaufort by traveling obscure waterways to avoid the French fleet anchored off Tybee Island. He arrived at Yamacraw bluff in time to discourage the British garrison and the Royal Governor in Savannah from surrendering. His reinforcements gave much needed aid to the British troops, and he was credited with lifting the siege. He was acclaimed a hero, recognized as such by both sides for his expertise and daring.

In 1950, the Georgia Historical Society received bone fragments from Maitland's right arm from the 15th Earl of Lauderdale, Ian Colin Maitland. They, consisting of four small ivory-like slivers, are preserved there as relics. Unfortunately, there is no explanation or document available relating the reason they were sent to the Historical Society.

But the Maitland story is not finished. In 1980 a team consisting of Dr. Preston Russell, a local pathologist, two professional historians, five archaeology students, and four children, received the necessary permission to open the Graham vault once more in order to determine if the remains of John Maitland were indeed entombed there.

On an autumn morning in October, they opened the vault

and began the search for John Maitland. Upon first entering the vault, they noticed the debris left behind when the Greene remains were removed. On their right were the pieces of coffin and bones of Robert Scott, identified by a tarnished coffin plate. Upon excavating in the far right corner they eventually discovered human remains — the bones of John Maitland. Identification was made on the basis of the missing right arm and other forensic clues. These bones were carefully removed and placed in an appropriate container.

As the excavators were preparing to leave the vault, a fourteen year old student by the name of John Jennings made a discovery on the wall of the vault. It was the letter "M" carved into the brickwork. This seemed to be the clinching argument that they had indeed found Maitland. The vault was once again sealed, leaving only the remains of Robert Scott inside.

During the summer of 1981, Dr. Russell and his wife returned John Maitland's remains to his ancestral home in Scotland. There they were placed in the Lauderdale vault in St. Mary's Cathedral in Haddington, along with a bronze plaque from the Georgia Historical Society. Thus, John Maitland returned home after more than 200 years in America.

BUTTON GWINNETT

The imposing Greek temple memorial to Button Gwinnett, Georgia signer of the Declaration of Independence, gives little indication of how it came into being. To fully appreciate its presence in Colonial Cemetery, we must first examine the person whom it honors.

Button Gwinnett was born in 1735 in Gloucestershire, England. He came to Georgia from Charleston sometime before Seprember of 1765 with his wife Ann and his daughter Elizabeth Ann. The family established a plantation on St. Catherine's Island. An article in the 1765 *Georgia Gazette* advertised that Button Gwinnett, a Savannah Merchant, had various household items, including Irish linen, medicines, herbs, butter, cheese, tin ware, and earthenware goods for sale. By 1770, Button Gwinnett had reached a level of some prominence in the Georgia colony. He served as a justice for St. John's Parish, using the designation of Esquire after his name.

When conflict arose between the colonies and England, Button Gwinnett cast his lot with the Americans. He went to the Continental Congress as a representative from St. John's Parish, and he signed the Declaration of Independence as one of the three signers from Georgia.

Gwinnett helped write the first constitution for the state of Georgia, and he succeeded Archibald Bulloch in 1777 as President of Georgia. It was during this period that Gwinnett and Lachlan McIntosh clashed over a statement Gwinnett made regarding McIntosh's brother. According to various accounts of the event in question, Button Gwinnett, then President of Georgia, ordered the arrest of Lachlan McIntosh's brother, George McIntosh, on charges of treason. With the charge of treason hanging over his brother, General Lachlan McIntosh was relieved of his command of the Georgia troops.

Both McIntosh and Gwinnett took their cases to the Assembly of Georgia in Savannah, which ruled in favor of Gwinnett. Angered by this decision, General McIntosh called Gwinnett, "a scoundrel and a lying rascal". In response to this slur on his character, Button Gwinnett challenged McIntosh to a duel which was fought on the 16th of May, 1777. While the exact location of this famous duel is not recorded anywhere, many historians believe that it probably took place out on what is today, Wheaton Street, near where the W. J. Bremer Company is today.

Major Joseph Habersham acted as a second for General McIntosh, while George Wells was Gwinnett's second. The two men faced each other at a distance of about ten paces, and fired. Both men were wounded in the leg; satisfaction was declared by both men, who were then taken to their homes to have their wounds treated. Button Gwinnett had taken the bullet just above his left knee; McIntosh's wound was in the thick part of his thigh. On May 28, 1777, Button Gwinnett died of gangrene which had developed in his wounded leg. He was buried with appropriate ceremonies in the old burying ground.

Elizabeth Ann Gwinnett went to Charleston, South Carolina

to school, and it was there that she married Peter Belin of Santee in 1779. Mrs. Ann Gwinnett died during this time, and it is likely that Elizabeth Gwinnett Belin also died about this time, as all trace of her seems to vanish. Thus, Button Gwinnett left no descendants, and his property was sold to satisfy his debts.

Arthur J. Funk, local State Representative and amateur historian, initiated a movement to locate the remains of Button Gwinnett in 1957. He and a team of archaeologists excavated a site in the cemetery which seemed the likely location of Gwinnett's remains. This investigation uncovered the remains of a man with an injured left femur. A man's queue of hair was also discovered beneath the skull. Great debate then followed at the annual Georgia Historical Society meeting in February as to whether or not the remains of Button Gwinnett had been found.

In the meantime, the city of Augusta was clamoring to bring Gwinnett's bones there to be interred under an appropriate monument, along with Lyman Hall and George Walton, Georgia's other two signers of the Declaration of Independence. Having identified the remains as those of Button Gwinnett, A. J. Funk kept the bones in a copper-lined box at his home on Isle of Hope.

These remains were buried at the monument site in September of 1964 at an unpublicized ceremony, with the rector of St. John's Episcopal Church reciting the recommital prayer of the church. In October of 1964, the completed monument was officially unveiled amid much ceremony. The bronze inscriptional tablet included a facsimile of Button Gwinnett's signature which is considered the rarest of signatures by autograph collectors. The monument stands on the supposed site of Gwinnett's burial as a memorial to a man who rose from relative obscurity to a place of prominence in the annals of this state and this country.

The Button Gwinnett memorial

The enclosure containing the remains of General Lachlan
McIntosh, along with other family members.

GENERAL LACHLAN McINTOSH

When General Oglethorpe established the Georgia colony, one of its purposes was to provide a buffer between the English colonies to the north and the Spanish settlements in Florida to the south. To reinforce this protection, he invited a group of one hundred thirty Scottish highlanders, led by John Mohr McIntosh, to come to Georgia and establish a settlement on the Altamaha River.

Among these Scots were McIntosh's sons, William, the older, and Lachlan who was born in 1727, near Inverness, Scotland. They established a town near the mouth of the Altamaha River and named it New Inverness. This town became what is today, Darien, Georgia.

John Mohr McIntosh took part in an expedition into Florida with Oglethorpe. He was captured by the Spanish in St. Augustine, and when Oglethorpe was unable to exchange him, was then taken to Spain where he was held for a number of years. Young Lachlan was thirteen years old at the time.

General Oglethorpe placed William and Lachlan McIntosh in his regiment as cadets. When Oglethorpe was recalled to England because of the threat there of a Stuart uprising, William and Lachlan hid on Oglethorpe's ships as stowaways, intending to return to Scotland to fight for the Stuart cause. They were discovered, however, and Oglethorpe convinced them of the hopelessness of the Stuart cause and received their pledge that they would remain in the colonies.

Lachlan McIntosh later went to Charleston and completed his education in business. Preferring the outdoors, he returned to Georgia where he married and began a career as a land surveyor.

When the rebellion of the colonies against English rule began, McIntosh declared that his loyalties were with the American colonies. When the Continental Congress called for the raising of troops to protect Georgia, Lachlan McIntosh became colonel of the Georgia battalion. He remained in service until the end of the Revolution, attaining the rank of Brigadier General.

On May 16, 1777, General McIntosh and President of Georgia, Button Gwinnett, met on the field of honor on the outskirts of Savannah. The two men had long been bitter opponents in the political arena, and, when Gwinnett ordered an expedition into Florida, he ignored McIntosh as the commanding officer, appointed subordinates to lead the forces, and set himself as commander of those troops. Gwinnett justified his decisions in that George McIntosh had been accused of treason, unjustly as it turned out, and felt that Lachlan McIntosh was tainted by the accusation against his brother. This quarrel ended with Gwinnett challenging McIntosh to a duel.

Both men were wounded in the leg, but Gwinnett's turned gangrenous and he died some days later. McIntosh's wound, while not fatal, required him to convalesce for some time. When news of Gwinnett's death came to him, he turned himself in to authorities and was released on bond. He won an acquittal, but was censured by many. He served with General Washington at Valley Forge and became well-respected in the Revolutionary Army.

After the war, he returned to Savannah and lived in the house at 110 East Oglethorpe Avenue. Lachlan McIntosh died February 20, 1806, at the age of seventy-nine. He was buried in a brick vault near the Abercorn Street walk in the old cemetery. Sometime in the early 1900's, the vault apparently had deteriorated, either through vandalism and/or passage of time. Whatever the reason, McIntosh's remains, along with those of other family members, were removed from the vault and buried in the ground near the Screven vault. An iron fence surrounds the site, and stones mark the graves of various family members buried there.

GENERAL SAMUEL ELBERT

To the left of the entrance and down near the fence on Oglethorpe Avenue is an austere gray granite box tomb with the name ELBERT deeply engraved in the tablet set in one end. This tomb was erected in 1924. Within the tomb are interred the remains of Samuel Elbert and his wife Elizabeth Rae. They were interred there March 11, 1924.

Samuel Elbert was born about 1740 in St. William's Parish, South Carolina. He was the son of William and Sarah Elbert who came from England to South Carolina in 1732. William Elbert was a Baptist minister in St. William's Parish, but he and Sarah moved to Savannah after the birth of Samuel. William Elbert died in 1754 when Samuel was just fourteen years old.

The orphan boy became a successful merchant, and a leading citizen in Savannah. In 1769 he married Elizabeth Rae, daughter of John Rae, a business partner. They raised six children on their plantation known as Rae's Hall, a few miles upriver from Savannah.

Samuel Elbert served his country well. His military career included colonial service with royal troops, but when America rebelled against English rule, he cast his lot with the American forces. He saw service under General Washington, and rose to the rank of Brigadier General in the Continental Army, along with Lachlan McIntosh, the only two officers to attain this rank. In 1785, Elbert became governor of Georgia.. He was also a trustee of Chatham Academy in 1788, and Sheriff of Chatham County.

The *Georgia Gazette,* dated November 6, 1788, gave the following account:

> Savannah. November 6. Died. Last Saturday after a lingering sickness, aged 48 years, Samuel Elbert, Esq., Major general of the militia of this state, vice president of the Society of the Cincinnati, and Sheriff of Chatham. His death was announced by the discharge of minute guns and the colours of Fort Wayne and vessels in port displayed at half mast... Buried in the family burial place on the Mount at Rae's Hall.

Four years later, the *Georgia Gazette* ran the following notice:

> Savannah. January 26, 1792. Died. At Great Ogeechee. Mrs. Elizabeth Elbert, widow of General Samuel Elbert.

She, too, was buried in the family graveyard on the Mount at Rae's Hall.

The "Mount" referred to in the death notices was in actuality a large Indian mound, about fifteen feet high, with a base diameter of about fifty-five feet. It was located about five miles upriver on a bluff near where Pipemaker's Creek or Canal joins the Savannah

River, and predated Oglethorpe's arrival in Georgia by so many years that the Yamacraws living in the area in 1733 avoided it entirely because of "spirits". It was not part of their heritage or culture. In 1736 Moravian missionaries built the first Protestant school building on its summit and named the resulting settlement," Irene." The Rae family acquired the property as part of their plantation in 1740. They used the "Mount", as they called it, as the family burial ground.

The modern granite box tomb of Samuel Elbert and his wife, Elizabeth Rae

In the late 1890's, Clarence B. Moore made a limited archaeological survey of the site, and published his findings in a book entitled, *Certain Aboriginal Mounds, Etc.*, in 1899. The site became known as the Irene Indian Mound. A later archaeological investigation revealed that the mound actually consisted of tiers with temples. The investigation also determined that there were approximately 265 Indian burials in the mound. In 1907, the Chatham County Engineering Department removed the entire north side of the mound in order to obtain fill dirt to build floodgates at the mouth of Pipemaker's Creek.

During the second decade of the 1900's, a group of young boys from several prominent Savannah families discovered a reference to the Indian mound and decided to try to locate the site in order to collect arrowheads and other Indian relics. On their first expedition, they not only located the mound, but also discovered bones sticking out of a cut made by the county engineers.

Their discovery included not only bones, but also coffin nails and handles. By this time, they were reasonably certain that the remains were not those of Indian burials.

On a return trip, they discovered that someone had collected the remaining bones, wrapped them in a handkerchief, placed them back in the hole the boys had dug, and covered them with Spanish moss. The boys continued to dig, finding more coffin handles, nails, and another skeleton. Two of the boys took some of the bones home. On their last trip to the site, they found that all of the bones had been removed. A few days later the local newspaper carried an article, "Vandals Desecrate the Grave of General Elbert". Though scared, eventually the boys took the bones they had taken to the Georgia Historical Society at Hodgson Hall and handed them over to Mr. William Harden, who was the librarian for the society. Apparently the bones remained in the librarian's desk for several years.

Mr. Thomas P. Ravenel, who was then first vice-president of the Georgia chapter of the Sons of the Revolution, and was in the habit of walking on the Rae's Hall Plantation site, came home one night with a handkerchief in which were wrapped human bones. He turned these bones over to General Robert J. Travis, who was also an officer in the Sons of the Revolution. Travis placed the bones in his desk drawer where they remained for several years while he attempted to prove that they were the bones of Samuel Elbert.

Mr. Thomas Gamble, in a historical sketch for the Sons of the Revolution, wrote:

> Considerable time was necessarily consumed in the examination of the records and the final locations of the mound, and the exhumation of the remains of General Elbert. The bones were placed in the custody of General Travis. The skull was missing, and it was later recalled that the Chatham County forces, in removing dirt from the mound for filling purposes, had uncovered a skull, which been kept in the County Commissioner's office until carried away by a relic hunter. Another skeleton, presumably that of his wife, found alongside the remains of General Elbert, was left in the custody of William Harden. These remains were re-interred in the Colonial Cemetery and a granite tomb placed over the grave.

The re-interment took place March 10, 1924, amid great ceremony. According to the newspaper account of the event, a gun salute was fired in Forsyth Park, the rector of Christ Church led a prayer of invocation for the soul of General Elbert, and a large funeral cortege moved slowly down Liberty Street while the guns boomed in Forsyth Park. A full military escort marched along behind. At Colonial Cemetery, speeches were made by various dignitaries. A final prayer of recommittal was offered by the Reverend David Cady Wright as the remains, in a flag- draped casket, were placed in the tomb, and "Taps" were sounded. Thus, General Samuel Elbert and his wife Elizabeth were interred in the Old Burying ground where many of their old acquaintances and friends rested.

Whether the bones which now rest in the vault were actually those of Elbert and his wife, or whether they belonged to the Rae family, or were perhaps even Indian, was a thorny question that was discussed by a number of prominent and learned individuals. One of the young boys who had taken some bones home from the mound, eventually discarded them in a trash can which was emptied and the contents removed to the city dump. Whose bones were these? It is unlikely that an answer will be forthcoming.

The old Irene Indian Mound no longer exists, being leveled and built upon by the Georgia Ports Authority. Warehouses and a paved road cover the site where a large box containing the remains of what is believed to be at least fifteen members of the Rae family is buried. They were buried on the site for safekeeping, but the upheavals of World War II, and subsequent construction on the site have eradicated all trace of this colonial family.

ARCHIBALD BULLOCH

A square white marble column, topped with an urn, marks the purported grave of an ancestor of Theodore Roosevelt. Some refer to it as the "serpent tomb", so called because of the carving on its sides. A serpent with its tail in its mouth is an ancient symbol of eternity. The serpent depicted on this monument, however, appears to be a rattlesnake, merely coiled in a circle. The symbolism seems to indicate a different meaning which must remain a mystery.

The mysterious "Serpent" monument that marks
the reputed grave of Archibald Bulloch.

For many years this obelisk was unmarked, with only the serpents
to evoke a sense of the mysterious. Numerous stories circulated over
the years regarding the strangely carved, unmarked stone.

Some suggested that it marked the grave of a young man who
died as a result of a duel, and who had requested that his name
not be inscribed on his tomb. Others believed that it was the
grave of a suicide, while some locals declared that it was Button
Gwinnett's tomb.

In 1921, however, such speculations ceased when Miss Emma
Bulloch of Washington, Georgia, had the monument engraved
with the inscription it bears today, honoring Archibald Bulloch,
the first president of Georgia, 1776-1777.

Archibald Bulloch was born in Charleston, South Carolina, in
1730. He died in Savannah in 1777, a patriot, soldier, and states-
man. He was the great grandfather of Mittie Bulloch, the mother
of Theodore Roosevelt. Because Bulloch died during the
Revolutionary War, his grave was at first left unmarked. According

to Emma Bulloch, the family always intended to have the stone inscribed, and thus, this intention was finally realized in 1921. However, it would not be long before this claim would be questioned.

In 1929, Morton Kirk Moore of Charleston, South Carolina, a former resident of Savannah, was visiting the city and ventured into Colonial Cemetery. He disputed the idea that this stone marked the grave of Archibald Bulloch. He believed that Bulloch was buried either in Roswell, or more likely in the Midway cemetery, there being an unidentified monument in a prominent location in that cemetery.

According to Mr. Moore, the stone originally stood in the southwest section of the cemetery in the 1880's. He stated that when the cemetery opened as a park, and a walk was built through to the southwest corner, it became necessary to move the stone to its present location. This stone was originally a plain box-shaped monument, with only the snake carvings on each side. The laborers who moved the stone, found the urn and cemented it to the top of the monument.

The true story, as presented by Moore, was that the monument had been erected for the son of a wealthy, prominent Savannah family. This young man joined a band of raiders who sided with the English during the Revolution. The raiders, known as the Pen Darvis band, ambushed and killed a Captain William Kirk at his plantation known as Black Swamp. A group of American patriots, led by Captain Schoolcraft, pursued the raiders, hanging those who were not killed in the capture. One of those was the young Savannahian who had joined the Pen Darvis band.

Still one other account, taken from a paper by Jane Judge, relates that the monument marked the grave of a suicide, believed to be a descendant of Archibald Bulloch. It was said to have been brought secretly from England where it was carved under secret orders. It was then erected in the dead of night by unknown workmen.

It may never be known for certain who, if anyone, lies beneath the monument, but today it stands, still shrouded in mystery, as a memorial to Georgia's first president, Archibald Bulloch.

WILLIAM SCARBROUGH

William Scarbrough was born February 18, 1776, near Beaufort, South Carolina. He was the son of a wealthy planter, and a descendant of an early New England Puritan, John Cotton. He was educated in England, and also at the University of Edinburgh in Scotland. Scarbrough came to Savannah about 1798. Because of his education abroad, he had made many foreign connections. This background, no doubt, led to his being appointed Vice-Consul for Denmark for all the Georgia ports in 1802.

William Scarbrough married Julia Bernard of Wilmington, North Carolina, about 1805.

She was so noted in Savannah society for her determination to be a society leader and for her elaborate parties and genteel airs, that she was locally referred to as the "Countess". She was a close friend of Robert Mackay of Savannah.

Scarbrough was one of a group of Savannah businessmen known as the "Merchant Princes", men of wealth who were leaders in civic affairs as well as commercial endeavors. In 1818, William Scarbrough became one of the principal promoters and investors in the plan to order an ocean-going steamship. This combination steam and sailing vessel was intended for trans-Atlantic service. It was to be constructed in New York, and would be named *Savannah*.

This vessel would be commanded by Captain Moses Rogers, who had come to Savannah from Connecticut. Other local investors included Archibald Bulloch, Andrew Low, Isaac Minis, Robert and James Habersham, and Benjamin Burroughs.

The *Savannah* arrived in Savannah in April of 1819 from New York. In May of that same year, newly-elected President James Monroe came to Savannah, and was a guest of William Scarbrough's in the just-completed Scarbrough mansion at 41 West Broad Street. Scarbrough had commissioned the English architect William Jay to design this house, and it was completed just in time for Monroe's visit to Savannah, which lasted five days. President Monroe stayed in the Scarbrough mansion which had been hastily fitted with furniture borrowed from neighbors.

On May 12, 1819, President Monroe, along with a number of city officials took a short trip to Tybee on board the *Savannah*. The next day, May 20, the *Savannah* sailed for Liverpool, England. She arrived in Liverpool twenty-nine days later, the first steam-powered ship to cross the Atlantic.

Unfortunately, the promoters of the *Savannah* were unable to interest commercial shippers in utilizing steamships to transport goods. While the maiden voyage proved the feasibility of trans-Atlantic steamships, the European merchants merely considered the *Savannah* a novelty, and were not interested in her commercial potential.

The *Savannah* returned to America where she was eventually stripped of her engine, and put into service as a sailing ship. She ran aground off Long Island, New York in 1821, and was destroyed.

In the meantime, the city of Savannah had been devastated by a multi-million dollar fire that had destroyed the financial and business center of the city, as well as hundreds of houses. These losses, as well as the failure of the *Savannah* to attract commercial attention, resulted in financial ruin for William Scarbrough who had invested so much in the venture. He lost the mansion on West Broad Street in bankruptcy proceedings, but it was purchased by Robert Isaac, a relative who allowed him to continue living there. He died in New York on June 11, 1838, at the age of sixty-three. His remains were brought to Savannah and interred in the Scarbrough family vault on June 15, 1839. His wife, Julia, died December 16, 1851.

The Scarbrough vault also contains the remains of Scarbrough's daughter, Lucy, who married Horace Sistare. Lucy Scarbrough Sistare died in 1840, at the age of twenty-eight. Four of the Sistare children are also interred here. Only one of these children lived more than one year: Julia, who died from scarlet fever in 1840, at the age of four years and six months. Robert Isaac, a native of Scotland, and a Scarbrough relative, is also entombed here.

WILLIAM LEIGH PIERCE

No stone marks the grave of William Leigh Pierce. It was destroyed long ago. Indeed, the site of this man's grave is unknown. What is known is that he is buried in Colonial Park Cemetery.

William Leigh Pierce was born in Virginia in 1740. In 1776, he was commissioned as captain in the First Continental Artillery. He served as an aide-de-camp to General Nathanael Greene, participating in a number of significant battles during the American Revolution. By the close of the war he had attained the rank of major.

In 1783 Pierce married Charlotte Fenwick. They had three sons, only one of whom survived childhood. This son, also named William Leigh Pierce, graduated from Princeton, but died in 1815 of typhus fever.

At the end of the Revolution, Pierce moved to Savannah and established a mercantile business, which proved to be unsuccessful. He was a prominent member of Savannah society, and served as vice-president of the Society of the Cincinnati in Georgia. He was also a member of the Union Society which was responsible for the maintenance of Bethesda Orphanage, and also a member of Solomon's Lodge No. 1, F.& A. M.

Pierce represented Georgia in the Continental Congress of 1786 and 1787. As such, he took part in framing the new Constitution, although because he was called to New York on business, he was not present to sign the new Constitution of the United States.

William Leigh Pierce, the man who did not sign the Constitution of the United States, died December 10, 1789, at the age of forty-nine. He was buried in the old burying ground, carried to his grave by the Society of the Cincinnati, the Union Society, and members of Solomon's Lodge. The Chatham Artillery fired a salute along the funeral route. His widow Charlotte married Ebeneezer Jackson in 1792, and the Pierce family passed out of existence.

ABBE JEAN BAPTISTE LEMOINE

Little is known about this shadowy figure who fled the French Revolution and ended up in Savannah. From the available information one learns that he was once the Cure of Marly Le Roi in France. It is highly likely that he was an aristocrat by birth. From a letter written by a Father LeMercier who was sent to Savannah in 1796 by Archbishop John Carroll of Baltimore, we learn that Father LeMoine was either sent to Savannah by the archbishop, or he came to Savannah directly from France. There are some references that indicate that he began his ministry in a village about fifty miles above Augusta called Maryland.

Another source suggests that Father LeMoine may have come to Savannah from the West Indies and begun his work in Florida This may be of some relevance when one reads of the Spanish sailors' part in the funeral of the priest in Savannah in 1794.

The brick vault which purports to be the resting place of the Abbe LeMoine, the first Roman Catholic priest in Savannah.

An interesting statement by Father John O'Connell, writing about his younger days as a priest in this country, mentions a Mass at which he officiated in St. Mary's, Georgia, in the 1840's, where he used an ancient chalice engraved with the name of a Father Moine. He adds that this priest "officiated on the islands" and in Florida at the close of the last century. At any rate, while the time of LeMoine's arrival here is not known, he ministered to the very small group of Catholics, mostly French refugees, who were in Savannah at that time.

A notice in the *Georgia Gazette,* dated November 20, 1794, states, "Died. The Rev. Mr. Lemoyne. Mr. Rodolph Strohacker."

Mr. Strohacker was a butcher in Savannah and a member of the Lutheran church. He and his wife Elizabeth evidently had a boarding house on Broughton Street, or owned some houses which they rented, as they are mentioned in a number of notices in early newspapers. It is possible that they were LeMoine's landlords.

An agent for the French Consul in Savannah at that time by the name of Francis Courvoisie, and Thomas Dechenaux, a friend of Father LeMoine, took an inventory of the priest's possessions and searched for a will which Father LeMoine had mentioned to Dechenaux. No will was found, and the French consul took charge of Father LeMoine's possessions, including some items which were actually church property. Several notices in the *Gazette* appeared at intervals, announcing the sale of LeMoine's possessions, "consisting of table linens, wearing apparel, sheets, etc." Later issues of the *Gazette* list LeMoine's name as having unclaimed mail in the post office.

Father LeMercier arrived in Savannah in October of 1796, having been sent here by Bishop John Carroll of Baltimore. He wrote to the bishop, informing him that LeMoine was dead, and that the French consul had seized all of LeMoine's possessions, including church property and a gold watch. LeMercier wrote that he intended to recover as many of the possessions as possible and turn them over to the bishop.

He also wrote that a Spanish vessel was in port at the time of LeMoine's death, as was a French privateer. The Spaniards had insisted upon a proper funeral, with LeMoine's body clothed in his vestments and a cloth over his face. This was done, but when the corpse was placed in its grave and only two or three inches of dirt covered the body, the French soldiers who were present began singing *Le Marseille,* and a riot broke out. The French soldiers then went to the house where LeMoine had lived and tore a cross off of his door, breaking it, and shouting obscenities and blasphemies.

Father LeMercier concluded his account of the funeral by stating that he intended to go to Father LeMoine's grave and perform the proper funeral ceremonies before he left Savannah. Thus LeMoine finally received the burial rites of the church two years after his death.

The western section of the burial ground was used by the Catholics. At the end of each ten-year period, the graves were opened to receive new burials. According to the Reverend J. J. O'Connell. O. S. B., writing in 1844 in his *Catholicity in the Carolinas and Georgia*, this practice left the entire surface covered with the debris of human remains. He says that the old families had vaults which protected their deceased relatives, but the overcrowding of the single burials necessitated this inhuman but unavoidable invasion.

Today, a large red brick vault interrupts the iron fence on Abercorn Street. A metal plaque affixed to the vault pays tribute to Abbe Jean Baptiste LeMoine, Cure of Marly Le Roi, France, and the first English-speaking Catholic priest in Savannah, who died in 1794.

After much searching of records, I finally discovered that the Trustees' Garden Club, who worked on a restoration and beautification project from about 1967 until 1970, placed the plaque there.

Is Father LeMoine's body in that vault? Whose vault was it? LeMoine is not listed in *Some Early Epitaphs in Georgia,* which indicates that there was no identifying marker for him in 1924. Why were the priest's remains not removed to Catholic Cemetery when it opened in 1853, when there were between a hundred sixty and two hundred removals made to Catholic Cemetery?

A search in the Catholic Archives of the Diocese of Savannah did not answer these questions. Indeed, many of the local church officials would like these questions answered also.

In speaking with some members of the Trustees' Garden Club who had participated in the beautification project, I was unable to locate anyone who could tell me how they knew about LeMoine and his grave site, and were thus able to place a plaque there.

Somewhere there are answers, but in the meantime, Father LeMoine remains somewhat of a mystery.

EDWARD GREENE MALBONE

Edward Greene Malbone, son of General John Malbone and Patience Greene, was born in Newport, Rhode Island, in August of 1777. He was related to General Nathaniel Greene. At an early age Malbone exhibited artistic talents. He left home in 1794 to begin his career in Providence, Rhode Island. From there he traveled to Boston and Philadelphia, as well as to other cities along the east coast.

A self-taught painter, Malbone quickly developed a talent for painting miniatures on ivory. Using thin transparent watercolors, he was able to obtain delicate flesh tones and textures. In 1797, he painted a self-portrait of himself in oils. This painting was owned by the Corcoran Gallery of Art in Washington, D. C. A copy of this portrait was later made and presented to the Telfair Gallery of Arts and Sciences in Savannah.

In 1800, Malbone came to Charleston. While in Charleston, he painted miniatures of many of the prominent Charleston families, including the Pinckneys, Manigaults, Rutledges, Middletons, Hugers, Heywards, and Poinsetts. The following year he went to Europe, and studied at the Royal Academy in London. At some point in his travels, Malbone contracted tuberculosis, or consumption, as it was then called.

Returning to America, he came to Savannah, where he had relatives, in hope that the warm climate would be beneficial to his health. He lived with his cousin's family, the Robert Mackays, in their home on the northwest corner of Congress and Abercorn streets. While in Savannah, he painted a number of miniatures including George Washington Greene, son of Nathanael Greene, a kinsman of Malbone's. He also painted a miniature of Martha Washington Greene, a daughter of General Greene.

On May 7, 1807, Edward Greene Malbone died of consumption at his cousin Robert Mackay's house. He was twenty-nine years old at the time. He was buried in what is today Colonial Cemetery. In the twelve short years of his artistic career as a painter of miniatures, he painted between three and five hundred miniatures of both men and women, many of whom were famous in their own right.

In 1929, the National Gallery of Art hosted a special exhibit of one hundred and fifty miniatures painted by Edward Greene Malbone. The exhibit consisted mainly of Charleston miniatures, with some from Philadelphia and New York. Miniatures of the Savannah families are still owned by their descendants, including an unfinished painting of Robert Mackay.

INTERESTING GRAVESTONE SYMBOLISM

DOCTOR SAMUEL VICKERS
Born: 1755— Died: October 15, 1785

The stone that marks this grave is one of the older stones in the cemetery. It is a headstone made from reddish sandstone, and is incised with the figure of a winged soul wearing a curly wig or peruke.

This is a very good example of early gravestone artwork. It should be properly called a soul portrait as there is apparently some attempt to give it the distinctive attributes — the wig — of the person whose stone it marks.

The stone of Dr. Samuel Vickers shows a very good soul portrait.
Note the curly wig. This stone is New Jersey sandstone and is possibly
the work of Ebeneezer Price of New Jersey.

The inscription reads as follows:

Here lies interr'd the body of Doctr. Samuel Vickers, who departed this life Octor the 15th Anno Domini 1785 in the XXX year of his age. He was born in New Brunswick and received the honors of the College at Princeton in N. Jersey. This monument is erected to his memory by his affectionate brother. T.L.V.

It certainly must have come as a shock to many of Savannah's citizens to read the following item that appeared in the October issue of the *Georgia Gazette* in 1785, about this well-respected member of the city: "Last Saturday afternoon Dr. Samuel Vickers shot himself through the head with a pistol at Sharon plantation near this town while insane."

Sharon was a plantation about six miles from Savannah on Louisville Road. It was the home of Governor Edward Telfair.

One wonders what events in Dr. Vickers' life led to this tragedy.

EMILY C. THOMPSON
Born: 1808—Died: October 6th, 1813

EDWARD THOMPSON
Born: 1813— Died: November 22, 1828

This interesting headstone depicts a carved relief of a winged soul figure or perhaps a bat hovering over a broken cherry tree. The broken tree alludes to a life broken or cut down by death. The carving is set inside an oval. The bat figure is symbolic of the underworld, the night. This stone includes the inscription, "Peace to thy souls." The stone carver's name in the lower left corner is that of Andrew Gow of Savannah.

This stone fastened to the east wall is that of Moses Warner who died in 1819. It contains a number of fine examples of the stonecutter's art, including the classic urn.

The stone of Alexander Hamilton, a ship's carpenter who died in 1814, shows a youth holding a scythe in his left hand and what appears to be an hourlgass in his right. Both symbolize the inevitable triumph of death over youth. Hamilton was 25 years old.

Teleman Cuyler's stone depicts a soul portrait. Carved lotus blossoms adorn either side.

The fragment of Henrietta Burk's stone depicts a graceful willow tree draped over a funeral urn. Lilies are carved on either side.

There are two burials in this grave. The first is that of a five year- old girl, Emily Caroline Thompson. From existing records we know that she was born in Charleston, South Carolina, and was the daughter of Leslie Thompson, tailor. She was sick with worm fever for about three days before she died.

The stone of the two Thompson children is carved with a
bat, or possibly a soul in flight, set inside an oval. A broken
fruit tree, symbolizing life cut short before maturity, is
carved beneath the figure.

The second burial in this grave is that of Edward Thompson,
younger brother to Emily. He was fifteen years old, and was
employed as a clerk in Savannah. The Thompsons lived on
Congress Street. His death is recorded as being caused by an
inflammation of the bowels. This term was generally applied to
the condition we know as appendicitis.

JOHN J. EVANS
Born: ca. 1783— Died: Jan. 1813

This portion of John Evans' stone is affixed to the east wall of
the cemetery. It portrays a death's head, with crossed bones, the
entire carving set inside a circle. This symbol is a common funerary device used to represent death and our own mortality. While

this is the only figure of its kind found in Colonial Cemetery, this motif is very common in the New England states.

The death's head, complete with crossed bones, is carved on the stone of John J. Evans. Contrary to some "modern" interpretations, it does not mark a pirate's grave.

According to the *Annals of Georgia Mortuary Records,* John Evans was born in South Carolina and was a printer by trade. He had lived in Savannah for about three years prior to his death at the age of thirty from convulsions. He was a member of the Solomon Lodge, the Union Society, and also the Chatham Artillery. He was buried from his house on Broughton Street, survived by his widow and also a sister. Apparently he was a highly respected citizen.

The death's head reminds the observer that death comes to all, regardless of station in life.

CAPTAIN JOSEPH TROWBRIDGE
Born: ca. 1735— Died: December 17, 1790

The grave of Capt. Trowbridge is a little different from the other graves in Colonial Cemetery because it is an upright slate stone that has a matching foot stone. Stones with matching foot stones are rare in Colonial Cemetery. Both stones are engraved with a crowned soul figure. This particular motif, which is typical of a Connecticut stone carver, is symbolic of the soul's salvation. What little is known about Capt. Trowbridge is to be read from his tombstone which tells us that he was a native of New Haven, Connecticut, and that he was a much respected citizen who "sustained a long decline of health with calmness and resignation having maintained a reverence for the principles & maxims of the Christian religion."

Captain Joseph Trowbridge's stone shows a typical
winged soul, complete with a halo.

THEODORA ASH
Born: 1753— Died: February 17, 1770

The small stone which marks seventeen-year-old Theodora Ash is inscribed with a number of popular symbols of death and the grave. The opium poppies on either side represent the forgetfulness, or the sleep, of death. The hourglass and scythe both emphasize time running out, and the idea of the harvesting of a soul by death. A child's head adorns the top portion of the stone. We know this is a female because the laces of the bodice can be seen. The child's head is resting in its right hand, a traditional posture of sorrow. This particular carving is attributed to a stone carver by the name of John Bull, and is likely the only example of his work in Savannah that can be identified with any certainty.

The wording of the inscription is typical of colonial times. The spacing of the words on the stone is rather interesting. It reads:

HERE LYETH THE BODY OF
THEODORA ASH
WHO DEPARTED THIS LIFE
FEBRUARY THE 17TH, A. D. 1770
AGED 17 YEARS
IF INNONCE OR VIRTUE COULD SAVE
A LIVING MORTALL FROM THE GRAVE
THEODORA THOU HAD'ST NEVER DIED

There is a second matching stone in another location in the cemetery which is engraved with the name Theodora Ash, 1770. Quite probably this is the misplaced foot stone to the one above. Since this second stone is set quite solidly in the earth, perhaps it is yet another example of the handiwork of the Union troops in 1864.

Detail of the carving on the Theodora Ash stone.

MRS. GRACE BELCHER
Born: 1748— Died: January 14, 1793

This lovely upright headstone shows the familiar motif of the hourglass representing a life whose time has run out. The carving is very well done, and includes poppies on either side of the hourglass, symbolizing the sleep or forgetfulness of death. The arch symbolizes the departure from this life and the entrance into Heaven.

The inscription on this stone reads:

IN MEMORY OF
MRS. GRACE BELCHER
WIFE OF
MR. JAMES BELCHER
WHO DIED JAN. 14TH
1793 AGED 45 YEARS
ALSO JAMES PRYCE BELCHER
SON OF THE ABOVE PARENT
WHO DIED FEBY 21ST 1793
AGED 4 YEARS & 10 MONS

An hour glass with sands run out is found on the stone of Grace Carr Belcher. Poppies are carved on either side of the hourglass.

JOHN WILLIAM WAUDIN
Died September 25, 1794

This upright stone bears a winged soul figure, complete with hair, or perhaps a halo. John Waudin was the son of Dr. John Waudin, who was deceased, and he was apprenticed to a Savannah merchant named John Cunningham. It was Mr. Cunningham who had this stone erected. The *Georgia Gazette* of 1794 describes John Waudin as being "a youth beloved by all who knew him." The cause of his death was not given.

The John Waudin stone, erected by Savannah merchant John Cunningham

The John Kreiger stone, showing detailed relief carving of a willow, urn, and poppies.

JOHN KRIEGER
Born: 1755— Died: April 26, 1800

John Krieger's tombstone is a lovely example of detailed relief carving. It depicts a very nice willow tree, a classic symbol of sorrow. A larger funeral urn is also shown. The urn is decorated with a band of three rosettes or poppies. The poppies always suggest death as the sleep of forgetfulness, while the urn alludes to the ashes of the deceased.

ALEXANDER JAFFREY
Born: 1777— Died: April 9, 1810

Here lies the remains of

Alexander Jaffrey
(A native of Scotland)
Who departed this life
On the 9th of April, 1810
Aged 33 years

This stone shows a classic keystone arch, supported by Doric columns. Within the arch are Masonic emblems. The "ears" on either side of the stone contain a thistle, a Scottish emblem of remembrance. The entire design is in deep relief.

Alexander Jaffrey's name is mentioned in a number of documents as having a cotton machine house in Yamacraw. His death record indicates that he was born in Stirlingshire, Scotland. He was thirty-three when he died at and was buried from the poorhouse and hospital in Yamacraw.

Records state that he had lived in Savannah for several years and owned some property. The cause of death was given as a sore leg.

Thistles are carved on either "ear" of the Alexander Jaffrey stone. A Masonic emblem inside a gate is centered at the top of the stone.

The Rapp stone, mounted on the east wall, is carved with a number of interesting symbols. Here you see the willow tree bending over a casket on a bier. Sunbursts ornament either side of the inscription.

CHARLES F. RAPP
Born: October 20,1822— Died: October 28, 1822

CATHERINE RAPP
Born: 1794— Died: July 29, 1823
LOUISA RAPP
Born 1821— Died: October 2, 1823

This marker is affixed to the east wall of the cemetery. I included it because of its wealth of decorative carving in deep relief. It includes a very nice depiction of a willow tree, drooping over a casket resting on supports. Sunbursts decorate either side of the stone.

The Rapps lived on Drayton Street. *The Register of Deaths for Savannah* lists lockjaw as the cause of death for Charles, who was only eight days old when he died. One can only speculate as to how an eight-day-old infant could contract lockjaw. His mother, Catherine, who was a native of Sweden, died of country fever, as did her two year old daughter, Louisa. This was one of a number of fevers prevalent in the low country.

MRS. BRIDGET ROYSTON
Born: 1782— Died: October 28, 1806

Bridget Royston was the wife of Captain William Royston, a river pilot. She was born in Carrickonsuir, Ireland, in 1782. Mortuary records indicate that she died of a lung disorder or consumption, after an illness that lasted ten weeks. During this time she was unable to turn herself in bed. She died childless at the age of twenty-four, and was buried from her husband's house on Back Lane.

The stone which marks the Royston grave features an unusual engraving. Unfortunately, it does not photograph well because of its location and the condition of the stone. It depicts the figure of a man in knee breeches and a cutaway coat, with boots and a top hat. The figure, which likely represents Capt. Royston, the bereaved husband, is shown with bowed head, leaning on one elbow on a small monument which is adorned with a funeral urn. A cross is engraved on this small monument. The man is apparently weeping, as he holds a handkerchief to his eyes. The stone bears the familiar "May she rest in peace. Amen." at the end of the inscription.

The Bridget Royston stone was a difficult one to photograph, due to the lichens that covered the stone, and its location. However, it is possible to discern the figure of the of the bereaved husband.

MISS CAROLINE ELIZABETH JACQUELINE DeROSSIGNOL BELLEANSE
Born: November 4, 1807— Died: January 9, 1838

This imposing name is found on a large white marble slab near the fence on Abercorn Street. The top of the slab contains a coat of arms, presumably that of the Belleanse or DeRossignol family.

According to the stone, this lady was born at Gowvaines in the island of Hispaniola on November 4, 1807. She is described in the mortuary records as being the daughter of a great planter of Saint Domingue.

A description of this stone in *Some Early Epitaphs in Georgia* states that the slab was raised and resting on six brick pillars. Presently, the slab is flat on the ground, surrounded by partially buried bricks. The coat of arms at the top of the stone features a reclining dog below the shield. The inscription, *Requiescat X In Pace. Amen,* is included in the epitaph, which also states that she was descended from noble parents, and was held in very high regard by her friends and her parents.

It is very likely that her remains were removed to Catholic Cemetery. Because of the discrepancies in the birth and death dates, it is safe to assume that this is another of the many altered stones in the cemetery.

The Belleanese stone is carved with the family coat of arms. Note the figure of the reclining dog.

Photo by Stacey Yongue

INTRIGUING PEOPLE AND INSCRIPTIONS

In addition to the graves of important historical figures, Colonial Cemetery contains many interesting graves of the ordinary people who helped build Savannah. These people overcame all sorts of obstacles to establish a solid citizenry in the city. They came from many walks of life. They came for many different reasons. With them, they brought needed skills and knowledge to build a city, and eventually, a state and a nation. Many of them are long forgotten, but some remnants of their lives remain in the worn epitaphs that mark their resting places. Their stones tell of the sicknesses to which they fell prey. They tell of tragic accidents that befell them as they pursued their daily lives. Many of their descendants carry their names today.

This section deals with these individuals who struggled against the ravages of the unfamiliar fevers that plagued the low country; the mothers, often with their infants, who did not survive the birthing process; the children who succumbed to childhood diseases which are nearly unheard of today; and the ones who died while engaged in the day-to-day business of earning a living.

JAMES JOHNSTON
1738—1808

A large white marble slab marks the resting place of Georgia's first newspaper publisher and printer. An historical marker nearby tells us that Johnston was born in Scotland, but settled in Savannah in 1761. He was appointed public printer of the province. As a printer and publisher, he published the first issue of the *Georgia Gazette* in 1763. This newspaper circulated, with some interruptions, until 1802.

His sympathies with the royal government caused the press to close in 1776 until the British rule was restored in 1779. Johnston returned to Savannah and resumed publication of the *Gazette* as the *Royal Georgia Gazette* until Savannah fell into the hands of the American patriots. Johnston once again was forced to leave.

He was permitted to return to Savannah in 1783, after the Revolution. From that date on, the paper was known as the *Gazette of the State of Georgia.* His printing office was located on the south side of Broughton Street, east of Drayton.

James Johnston died October 4, 1808, at the age of seventy years.

ANNE GUERARD
Born : 1752— Died: July 11, 1793

As you enter the cemetery through the D.A.R. gate and look to the far right, near the iron fence, you will spot a large reddish brown slab which covers a brick vault. This site is one of the earlier grave sites in Colonial Cemetery. The epitaph informs us that this is the grave of Anne Guerard, a sincere Christian who died at the age of forty-one, just a few days after the birth of her fifteenth child! While we may be appalled at the idea of fifteen children, it would be well to remember that this figure may not take into account stillborn children. One wonders how many of these survived to the age of ten years.

The Anne Guerard stone, 1793. She died after giving birth to her fifteenth child.

The epitaph then continues with a warning or an admonition, written in the flowery prose of the day:

HOW LOV'D, HOW VALU'D ONCE AVAILS THEE NOT,
TO WHOM RELATED, OR BY WHOM BEGOT;
A HEAP OF DUST ALONE REMAINS OF THEE
TIS ALL THOU ART, AND ALL THE PROUD SHALL BE.

The remainder of the inscription reads:

The dead how sacred! Sacred is the dust
of this heav'n-labour'd form erect, divine
this heav'n assur'd, majestic robe of earth
He deign'd to wear, who hung the vast expanse
with azure bright, and cloth'd the sun in gold.

THOMAS VINCENT, ESQ.
Born: ca. 1728— Died: September 1767

This stone was not included in *Some Early Epitaphs in Georgia*. The stone is almost completely covered with a very long inscription, much of which is very difficult to read. I included it here because it is one of the very early ones, and also because this man was a Representative to the General Assembly of Savannah, and thus deserves some recognition.

His epitaph reads as follows:

Under this stone lies the body of Thomas Vincent, Esqr.
late Representative to the General Assembly of the
Town of Savannah, who departed this life the 31st
Sept. 1767 aged 39. He was one of the best Husbands
A most dutiful Son, sincere Friend and a kind Master
Esteemed by his Superiors
Beloved by his Equals
Lamented by the poor
A Zealous Asserter of Liberty, a check to tyranny
and a ——————Advocate to the Innocent, Helpless and
Oppressed—A Christian heart at the command of the Almighty
A Merchant

SUSANNAH GRAY
Born: June 2, 1792 — Died: July 26, 1812

According to a notice that appeared in *The Republican and Savannah Evening Ledger,* Tuesday, July 28. 1812, the following account is given for the death of Susannah Gray:

> Another melancholy instance of the effects of lightning occurred in this city on Sunday last, at the house of Mr. Thomas Dechenaux, in Broughton street, whereby a young lady, Miss Susan Gray, a native of new York, was almost instantaneously killed. Medical aid was had very speedily, but to no purpose. Miss Gray was an amiable young lady, and esteemed by all of her acquaintance. This is the second accident, the kind with which our city has been visited during the present month.

Annals of Georgia Mortuary Records tell us that Susannah Gray, age twenty-one, New York, Spinster, was the sister of a Mrs. Blanchard. Mr. Dechenaux, a member of Council and a merchant, was a native of Paris, France. His residence was at Broughton and Jefferson streets, and he and his wife had at least one daughter. It is likely that Susannah was visiting the Dechenaux daughter when her fatal accident occurred.

Her inscription quaintly informs us that she "departed this life by the will of God, being killed by lightning on the 26th, July 1812." It further notes that "Virtue and Modesty were her Adornments."

This is one of the stones on which the age of the deceased has been altered to read "aged 121 years and 1124 days," presumably by Union soldiers.

The stone of Susannah Gray not only states that her death was caused by lightning, but it also shows evidence of being altered during the Federal occupation of Savannah.

PEYTON LISBEY DENNIS WILSON
Born: 1829 — Died: October 1, 1835

MARY MADELINE DENNIS WILSON
Born: 1822 — Died: June 1, 1837

This grave contains the remains of two Wilson children. The small slab is slightly askew from the other Wilson stones which lie on either side. It is almost totally illegible today.

The little boy, Peyton Wilson, was only six years old when he died of convulsions. His family lived across the street from the cemetery, and according to the inscription, the child came out to the cemetery a week before he died and said, "Here. I want to be here." He was buried in this spot, according to his wishes.

Two years later the Wilson family suffered a second tragedy when a daughter, Mary, age fifteen, died of burns received in unusual circumstances, and was interred in the same grave as her brother.

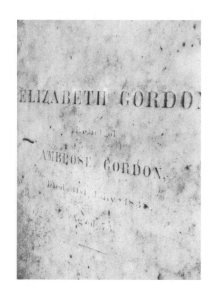

The damaged stone of William Ray

The Elizabeth Gordon ledger stone.

Her inscription states the incident:

> A CHRISTIAN MARTYR, HER BIBLE TOOK FIRE
> ON HER BREAST. A FEW PAINFUL HOURS & SHE
> SLEPT IN JESUS, TO WHOM SHE DEVOTED HER-
> SELF IN HER 9TH YEAR. SUCH TIMELY, BEAUTIFUL,
> THE LOVLINESS MEEKNESS TO HER GOD
> EXPRESSED; JOINING THE HOLY ARMY ABOVE,
> HER MESSAGE WAS I DIE WITH A GLORIOUS HOPE
> OF HEAVEN. "

One can only conjecture the cause of this unusual death. Perhaps she was reading her Bible by candlelight and the candle fell upon her, setting her clothing and Bible on fire. Perhaps it is an early account of spontaneous combustion! I could not locate a newspaper account of this tragedy, although I feel sure that this event would not have gone unnoticed.

To the left of this grave is that of another Wilson child, DANIEL STEWART LAFAYETTE WILSON, who died in

1833 of bilious fever. He was eight years old. According to his stone, and recorded in the death register, his final words were, "Now! I want to die now!"

The Wilson children were all extremely articulate for their age. Their mother, JANE DENNIS WILSON, is buried to the left of them. Her inscription enigmatically proclaims that she was "the first of three in her class."

HANNAH MOREL
Born May 20, 1776— Died April 5, 1790

If one looks closely at this large white slab which covers the resting place of a young girl, Miss Hannah Morel, one will note that a fall from her horse resulted in her untimely death.

The *Georgia Gazette,* dated April 8, 1790, reported the death of this young lady in the account that follows:

> On Monday last, as Miss Hannah Morel, daughter of the late John Morel, Esq., was riding on horseback, in the neighborhood of this city, with a party of young ladies and gentlemen, the horse took fright and ran away with her, she kept her seat for some time, but at length fell, and was taken lifeless in a few minutes, and by the time a surgeon could reach her, she expired.
>
> Thus perished, just as she was stepping into life, a young lady of most promising hopes, whose death, even in a common course, must have been affecting, but in such a way, is truly (sic) tragical.

At the time of her death, Hannah Morel was thirteen years old.

WILLIAM RAY
Born May, 1798— Died April 24, 1811

This lonely, much damaged, stone lies alone in a section of Colonial Cemetery that is often overlooked. It is a stone that has been broken and pieced back together several times, and much of the inscription is missing.

Young William Ray was the son of Captain Nathaniel Ray, master of the brig *America* which made many trips between Philadelphia and Savannah in the early 1800's. William went along as cabin boy. He was nearly thirteen years old when the *America* docked in Savannah in April of 1811. On the afternoon of April 24th William Ray fell to his death from the main topsail mast of the ship. The newspaper account of the day gave the following notice in the flowery language of the day:

> Died on Wednesday evening, the 24th instant on board the brig *America* Master WILLIAM RAY (son of Captain N. Ray), in the thirteenth year of his age. He was a fine promising youth & bid fair to be a useful member of society. His death was occasioned by a fall from the mast head and was as instantaneous as it was unexpected. Farewell blest spirit, thou hast flown to the realms of Immortality. in obedience to the will of the Supreme Disposer of human events, and, by thy early exit, escaped all sublunary affliction.

> "Fair was the flower and soft the eternal sky,
> Alas! we deemed no dangerous tempest night:
> When lo! the whirlwind's instantaneous gust,
> Left all thy beauties withering in the dust"

The marker on his grave, gives William's age as being 12 years, 11 months.

ELIZABETH GORDON
Born July 30, 1764— Died January 31, 1838

This simple marker reads:
        Elizabeth Gordon
        Relict of
        Ambrose Gordon
        Died 31st Jany. 1838
        Aged 73
The woman who lies beneath this plain stone was a most remarkable person. A widow at age thirty with six children to raise, she became a noted businesswoman in her own right.

Elizabeth Meade was born July 30, 1765, in Bedford County, Virginia. She married Ambrose Gordon June 4, 1787, in Augusta, Georgia. They had seven children, one of whom, a daughter, died at age three and was buried in Augusta. Ambrose died in 1804 near Augusta, and is buried in St. Paul's churchyard there. His will mentions his six children, his wife, land, and seven hundred acres on the Altamaha River, and in Camden County, Georgia.

Ambrose's widow moved into town in Augusta to a house on Greene Street. During the War of 1812 , Elizabeth proved herself to be an astute businesswoman. Seeking the highest possible price for her bales of cotton, she decided to run the American blockade at Savannah. Relying on gentlemen's chivalry not to fire on a lady, she floated down the Savannah River from Augusta, perched in a rocking chair atop her bales of cotton. According to family tradition, her risk paid off and she got a good price for her cotton. Perhaps her proven business aplomb is the reason she was appointed guardian for the minors and orphans of Ambrose Gordon in 1815.

About 1824, she moved to Savannah to live with her son, William Washington Gordon I, mayor of Savannah and founder of the Central of Georgia Railroad, and his wife, Sarah Anderson Stites Gordon. Elizabeth, or Betsy, as she was called, broke her hip in 1836, and for the last two years of her life was bedridden.

She died January 31, 1838, in the Wayne-Gordon house on the corner of Bull Street and Oglethorpe Avenue, and was buried in Colonial Cemetery. She was the great-grandmother of Juliette Gordon Low who founded the Girl Scouts of America in 1912 in Savannah.

WILLIAM GASTON
"Prince of Savannah Merchants"

When a visitor enters Savannah's famed Bonaventure Cemetery, he is immediately confronted with a white marble tomb with the name "GASTON TOMB" engraved at the top. This is the famed "Stranger's Tomb". What many do not know is that this tomb did not always stand where it does today. It originally was erected in Colonial Cemetery in 1847 as a memorial to a man much respected and highly admired as a successful businessman and a gracious host.

William Gaston was born about 1787, possibly in New Jersey. When he came to Savannah is not known, but once here he built a home on the corner of Habersham and Broughton streets.

In 1822, he became President of the Planters Bank in Savannah, a most prestigious position. He was one of the so-called "Merchant Princes" of Savannah. Gaston was widely known for his kindnesses, especially to strangers. It is said that Gaston, a bachelor, seldom sat down to a meal at his table alone.

In 1837, William Gaston made a trip to New York City. There on September 12, 1837, William Gaston died. When the news reached Savannah several days later, the bells of Independent Presbyterian Church and the City Exchange tolled to mourn his passing. A committee of prominent businessmen in the city proposed to build a tomb in the old cemetery in which to inter his remains. Plans were finalized in 1844, and the marble tomb was erected to house Gaston's remains and also the remains of any stranger who happened to die while in Savannah. Although this idea may seem a little strange to us, there are several factors that governed these actions.

It had been obvious for some years that the old cemetery was overcrowded. Travelers from other areas coming into Savannah were not acclimated to the weather, and were thus especially susceptible to the prevalent fevers that plagued the area on a seasonal basis.

The city, recognizing the crowded conditions of the cemetery, had passed an ordinance prohibiting non-residents from being buried there. Potter's field on the South Commons was where strangers were usually hastily buried when a relative could not be found to provide for their burial.

Since Gaston had been known for his kindness to strangers visiting or passing through Savannah, it was thought that a tomb such as the one proposed would provide a place for a body to be placed until a relative could be located. This would be a fitting tribute to William Gaston.

The William Gaston tomb, referred to as the "Strangers'
Tomb," at Bonaventure Cemetery in Savannah. This tomb
originally stood in Colonial Cemetery.

The tomb was erected and the remains of Gaston were brought
from New York and interred there in 1846. An ordinance was drafted
that provided the tomb as a holding or receiving vault for strangers
for a period of one year, at which time the remains of the stranger
would either have been claimed by kinsmen or removed for burial
in the common ground. Gaston himself was placed in a lead coffin
with an identifying silver coffin plate and placed in the tomb to per-
petuate the role in death that he had distinguished in life as the
epitome of Southern hospitality.

In 1864, Union soldiers broke open the tomb, but Gaston's
remains were not disturbed by them, most likely because they
had been bricked up within the tomb itself.

After the Civil War, a group of citizens fearful that the tomb
would be subject to vandalism and neglect, carefully dismantled
the tomb, and rebuilt it just inside the entrance to Bonaventure
Cemetery. Gaston's coffin, with his remains and those of two
others who were not identified, were replaced in the tomb.

WILLIAM BOWER WILLIAMSON
Born: Ca. 1728—- Died: February, 1762

The grave of William Bower Williamson, marked by an unimpressive gray slate stone, is the oldest known grave in Colonial Cemetery. Located to the left of the path from the main gate, it has been so damaged and vandalized over the years, that very little of it remains. Much of the inscription is missing. What is left of the stone is set upright near the red brick vault of the Hulse family.

The oldest marked grave in Colonial Cemetery, 1762.

JOHN TUCKER
Born: 1777— Died January 8, 1804

CORNELIUS LUDLUM
Born: 1775— Died: January 8, 1804

JOSEPH WHITE
Born: 1771— Died: January 8, 1804

This marble slab is decorated with Masonic symbols. These three natives of New Jersey all drowned together in the Savannah River. They were bricklayers who had come to Savannah to work.

According to an account of the tragedy, the three went out on the river in a rowboat which overturned. Being unable to swim, or perhaps caught in a current, they drowned. While parts of the inscription are illegible, we know from existing records that Ludlum and White both were married, but their families were in New Jersey.

Apparently they were friends, or perhaps even related. As they perished together, so they remained together in death. This is the only instance of a triple burial in the same grave on the same day in Colonial Cemetery.

ODREY MILLER
Born May, 1798 — Died July 13, 1831

A brown-stained slab marks the grave site of this intriguing gentleman. Odrey Miller was born in Scott County, Kentucky, in 1798. Being a native Kentuckian, it is not surprising that he earned a living as a horse trader. From the available accounts regarding Mr. Miller, he was well-liked and a rather popular individual, who had a number of friends and acquaintances in Savannah. Horse racing was a popular sport during this period of Savannah's history, and although there is no written account stating that Odrey Miller was a part of the horse racing scene, it is quite likely that he was.

In 1831, Odrey Miller and a local, popular politician by the name of Michael Brown apparently had some disagreements which resulted in a challenge. A duel was fought, and Odrey Miller died as the result of a bullet wound to his head. While an early newspaper account does not give the details of the duel, the following notice did appear:

> The friends and acquaintances of Odrey Miller, are requested to attend his funeral this afternoon (illegible) Johnson Square at four o'clock.

Friends of Odrey Miller placed a stone over his grave which named his murderer. Michael Brown's friends, presumably under cover of darkness, visited the cemetery and chiseled Brown's name from the stone. Thus the stone is read today as follows:

The stone of Odrey Miller, a Kentucky horse trader
who was killed in a duel in 1831.

To the Memory of
ODREY MILLER
a native of
Scott County, Kentucky
who died from a wound
inflicted by —————————————
on the 13th July, 1831
aged 33 years & 3 months

JACOB R. TAYLOR

The stone of Jacob R. Taylor, a young man of nineteen at the
time of his death, is one of those which is fastened to the east
wall. The inscription on the stone tells the tragic story of a young
man who came to Savannah from Philadelphia on board an
American ship. He hoped that the warmer climate would
improve his health. Unfortunately, events were soon to develop
which would dictate otherwise.

In November of 1811, there were two French privateers, *La
Francaise* and *La Vengeance,* docked in Savannah, ostensibly for
the purpose of buying supplies, but in reality, they were trying to

enlist men for their crews. The crews of these ships had a confrontation with some American sailors who disapproved of the recruitment of men by the French. According to the newspaper account of the event, some French sailors set fire to an American flag. Rioting broke out between the French and American sailors, and in the ensuing quarrel, three Americans were stabbed and killed.

The American sailors set fire to *La Francaise*. The mayor of Savannah then ordered the Savannah Volunteer Guards to take possession of *La Vengeance* and take it to safety.

Jacob R. Taylor's stone on the east wall.

However, some of the American sailors filled a small boat with tar and other combustible materials and towed it to *La Vengeance* in order to set that ship on fire. The Guards were unable to prevent this, and *La Vengeance* was also burned.

Several men on each side were killed, and nearly one hundred of the rioters were arrested. The mayor ordered the French consul to leave the city.

Taylor's rather large stone, which recounts the circumstances of his untimely death, presents a slightly different slant on the events which I have summarized here.

On the evening of November 14, 1811, Mr. Taylor strolled, unarmed, through the streets of Savannah. He was attacked by armed bandits who stabbed him to death. Investigation by authorities determined that Taylor's assailants belong to the crews of two French privateers, *La Vengeance* and *La Francaise,* which were in port at the time. There are indications that there had been some conflict between the French ships and the American ship on which Taylor had arrived in Savannah. Newspaper accounts of this event suggest that Taylor's comrades sought to retaliate for his death, thus inciting a riot with the crews of the French ships. Eventually the rioting was brought under control, and the instigators arrested and brought to trial.

The register of deaths in Savannah for that period of time gives a few more interesting details not reported in the newspaper. Taylor is listed as the second mate of the brig *Betty* of Philadelphia. He was stabbed during a fight in Yamacraw. Wounded at the same time as Taylor were two others. John Collins, presumably one of Taylor's shipmates, was also stabbed to death in the same affair. Cherie Shaddock was one of the crew members of the French privateer who also died of wounds he had received.

Thus, young Jacob Taylor, son of John R. Taylor of Philadelphia, ended his voyage in Savannah, a murder victim.

MAJOR EDWARD WHITE
Born: 1758— Died: January 9, 1812

This rather small headstone marks the grave of an officer of the Revolutionary Army. He was born in Brooklyn, Massachusetts, and came to Savannah about 1785. He was an important resident of Savannah for twenty-seven years, during which time he held a number of civic positions. He received a major's commission during the Revolution, and according to existing records, "acquitted himself with honor."

Major White owned property in the city, and at his death left a widow and four children.

At the time of his death, he was an Inspector for the Port of Savannah. Records show that his funeral was attended by the

Union Society, and Volunteer Corps of Savannah. The cause of death was given as an apoplectic fit. He was fifty-four years old at the time.

HANNAH G. SHEFTALL

About midway on the tabby walk that leads from Lincoln Street to Oglethorpe Avenue, just beside the walk itself, is an upright headstone bearing the name of Hannah G. Sheftall. She was the wife of Mordecai Sheftall, Jr. This is one of the Jewish burials in Colonial Park Cemetery, and what intrigues the reader is the sentiment expressed in the epitaph, which is more of a Christian idea than a Jewish one:

> In memory of
> Hannah G. Sheftall
> consort of
> Mordecai Sheftall, Jr.
> who was born
> on the 15th February
> 1803
> and departed this life
> on the 19th November
> 1834
> In thee we lose a friend sincere
> A loving wife, and mother dear
> Sincerely rest, thy sleeping dust,
> Till the last trump awakes the just.

INDIVIDUALS WHO MAY BE BURIED IN COLONIAL CEMETERY

It is obvious to even the most casual observer that there are large empty areas in the cemetery. Taking into account the removals that occurred when the other cemeteries opened in the city, there is still much space. When one looks at the number of stones fixed to the east wall, the number of unidentified vaults, and sites where a stone once stood, it is apparent that there must be unmarked grave sites. Indeed, an archaeological survey in August of 1998 identified over eight thousand unmarked grave sites. There are quite likely more than that number. Who are these people who lie here without a stone to mark their place today?

In reading through the death registers, knowing that some of those listed were prominent or well-known people in their day, and discounting those who occupy a mass grave, it is reasonable to conjecture that at least some of these people were interred here. The following sketches suggest some of the people who are believed to rest here in unmarked graves or tombs:

DR. MARY LAVINDER
Born: October 18, 1778—- Died November 19, 1845

Dr. Mary Lavinder is included in this work because the possibility is very great that she lies in Colonial Cemetery. She was a remarkable woman in an age when women were not expected to achieve recognition outside of marriage and family. Dr. Lavinder is probably the first woman doctor in Georgia. Her name appears in early mortuary records as an attending physician in a number of cases involving women or children.

Dr. Lavinder, or Miss Lavinder as she preferred to be addressed, was a spinster who was born in or near Savannah in

1778. She was the daughter of Benjamin Lavinder who owned a plantation at Burnside Island.

At any early age she became interested in pursuing a career as a medical practitioner, a highly unusual pursuit for an eighteenth century female. She probably began her career as a midwife, but sometime between 1810 and 1820, she went to Philadelphia to study obstetrics as a private student under Professor Thomas E. James at the University of Pennsylvania Medical School.

Miss Lavinder returned to Savannah in 1820 and set up an office on York Street where she specialized in the treatment of children and also in obstetrics. In that year, Savannah fell prey to three devastating catastrophes that had extensive consequences to the population. A widespread fire that year destroyed much of the city. This was followed by a hurricane that did further damage, and finally, in September, a major yellow fever epidemic struck the city. During these three disasters, Dr. Lavinder not only offered valuable medical service, but also carried much needed supplies to the poor, and to those who were victims of the disasters. She was not only a doctor, but a visiting nurse and social worker. Dr. Lavinder was an eccentric individual, with a forceful, but caring nature. She spent much of a large income on others who found themselves in dire circumstances.

Her reputation was such, that in 1818, she received an offer of a position in Boston to take over the practice of two prominent obstetricians there. Dr. Lavinder refused the offer and remained in Savannah. Although she did not have a medical degree, this was not unusual, as many doctors did not have a medical degree at that period of time.

Mary Lavinder was first a member of Independent Presbyterian Church, and then later, a member of First Presbyterian Church. She died suddenly on November 19, 1845. A search of *Some Early Epitaphs in Georgia* revealed that while Dr. Lavinder's brother, William, and his wife, Ann Mary Lavinder, were buried at Vernonburg, along with their daughter, Mary Catherine Lavinder, there is no record of Dr. Lavinder's burial there. Her parents, Benjamin and Rebecca Lavinder, may have been buried at Burnside Island near "Bewlie" (sic).

The only other record of a Lavinder burial was that of Miss

George Francis Lavinder,——years, who died of yellow fever in 1876, and was buried in White Bluff churchyard. Of Dr. Lavinder's burial, I could find no record. However, considering that she lived and worked on York Street, it is extremely likely that she would have been buried in the city.

PETER TONDEE
Died: 22 October 1775

Peter Tondee and his brother, Charles Tondee, came with their parents to Savannah from Switzerland in the early 1700's. Peter was sixteen, and his brother, Charles, was ten when their parents died. They were sent to live at Bethesda. In 1750, Peter Tondee, along with Benjamin Sheftall and Richard Milledge, founded the St. George's Club which later became the Union Society, the purpose of which was to provide financial aid to Bethesda in emergencies.

Peter Tondee had become quite skilled as a carpenter. This trade soon enabled him to acquire property. He married a widow, Lucy Mouse, from Acadia in Nova Scotia. In 1767, he became the inspector of lumber for the port of Savannah.

Tondee's tavern, located at the corner of what is today Whitaker and Broughton streets, became the center where the Sons of Liberty met, using the name "All Saints Quoits Club", or sometimes the Union Society as a cover for their meetings. On July 27, 1774, news reached Savannah that Britain had closed the port of Boston. In order to prevent trouble among the disgruntled citizenry, the royal governor, Sir James Wright, forbid the group to meet. The group convened as usual, however, and Peter Tondee stood at the door of his tavern and checked the credentials of each man who entered. More meetings followed as war became imminent.

Peter Tondee died nearly a year before Georgia's First Provincial Congress assembled at the tavern which Lucy Tondee now operated. It was here the raid on the powder magazine was planned, and then executed. Governor Wright ordered the arrest of the raiders and offered a reward, but no arrests were ever made. The next day the Liberty Pole with the Liberty flag was raised in front of Tondee's Tavern, and it was on August 10, 1776, in the tavern that the Declaration of Independence was read to the Council of Safety by Archibald Bulloch. The holiday in Savannah was celebrated with a mock funeral cortege, complete with an effigy of King George III in a coffin and a formal burial ceremony.

Peter Tondee's widow, Lucy Tondee, died September 22, 1785, in Savannah. Although there is no stone in Colonial Cemetery, it is safe to say that both are buried there. Several of their descendants are there. A daughter, Sally Tondee, married Frederick Schick in 1784. She most likely rests in the Schick family vault. Another descendant's stone, that of William Elon can be seen on the east wall. Another marker, that of Jane Elon, is yet another of Tondee's descendants.

INTERESTING OR NOTEWORTHY
DEATHS IN SAVANNAH

The information for the following accounts of deaths in or near Savannah were included in this book, primarily because of either the unusual circumstances surrounding their demise, or because they were noteworthy people whom I felt belonged in this work. While not all of these people are documented in some way as being interred in Colonial cemetery, it was reasonable to think that this was likely to be their place of burial, whether their grave was marked or not. A few may have been buried in Potter's Field. Most of this information came from printed death registers and old newspapers.

1. 1787 — John Stewart — This "gentleman" was executed for counterfeiting.

2. 1797 — Capt. John Moore — Capt. Moore died at sea on the *Shepherdess* bound for New York. His body was returned to Savannah and buried. He was a Savannah Alderman, and also Commander of Savannah Artillery Company.

3. 1775 — Joseph Ottolenghe, Esq. — Mr. Ottolenghe was Superintendent of the Silk Works

4. 1798 — Stephen F. Randolph — He died at the house of Joseph Berry in Savannah from an attack by Jeremiah and Patsy Vasteen at the house of Mrs. Reed at Yamacraw.

5. 1767 — William Sikes — Mr. Sikes was hanged January 9, 1767, in Savannah for horse stealing.

6. 1798 — Miss Susannah Gaffney — This lady drowned when the pilot boat, on which she was a passenger, capsized in a squall and sank. All were saved

except Miss Gaffney, who could have been saved but became hysterical and drowned.

7. 1798 — James Duncan — This unfortunate soul drowned while bathing at Cockspur.

8. 1801 — Hon. James Jones — A Representative in Congress, he practiced law in Savannah, and was a member of the Bar. He became a planter after his marriage. Jones was a delegate to the State Constitutional Convention. He was twice elected to Congress without opposition. He died January 19, 1801, in Savannah.

9. 1804 — John Wallace, Esq. — Mr. Wallace was the British Vice Consul for the State of Georgia. He died September 13, 1804, in Savannah.

10. 1804 — Hon. Joseph Clay — Judge Clay was Justice of the Inferior Court of Chatham County for 20 years. He was born in England in 1740 and came to America; at the beginning of the Revolution, he risked his fortune to fight with the Continental Army with General Greene.

11. 1818 — John C. Parisot — Mr. Parisot was a native of the Province of Lorraine, France. He went to Saint Domingue in 1789 where he printed a government gazette. He lost his wife and a child at sea on his way to the United States during the Haitian rebellion, but eventually came to Savannah with three of his children.

12. 1818 — Isaac Fell, Esq. — A native of Lancaster, England, he emigrated to America where he took part in the American Revolution, being wounded numerous times as well as being taken prisoner by the British. Mr. Fell came to Savannah in 1782, married, and had a family. Fell was a cabinet maker by trade, and he took an active part in public life in Savannah.

13. 1797 — Capt. Jeremiah Dickinson — This man drowned in the Savannah River while trying to save another person from drowning. He was fifty-seven years old. A large slab near the fence on Abercorn Street marks his grave site.

14. 1800 — Denis L. Cottineau Aude Kerloguen —

This Frenchman, a Lieutenant of the French navy, a Knight of the Royal and Military Order of St. Louis, commanded a warship, *Pallas,* of the United States during the American Revolution, and fought with John Paul Jones. His son, Achilles J. M. Cottineau de Kerloguen, lies with him also.

15. 1809 — Mrs. Anne McQueen — This marble slab covers the grave of one of the characters in Eugenia Price's Savannah quartet. Mrs. McQueen was the mother of Eliza Mackay. Nearby is Eliza's son John (Jack) Mackay. Eliza is buried in Laurel Grove.

16. 1810 — Major Charles Odingsells — A Patriot Soldier, he lies in a grave on the east side of the cemetery beneath a large slab. He died at the age of 36 at Skidaway Island. Also buried with him are his two children, Charles Spencer Odingsells, age 6, and Mary Susannah Odingsells, age 9, both of whom died in 1817.

17. 1815 — James Wilde, Esq. — This young man, age 22, was a District Paymaster of the 8th Regiment. He was killed in a duel with Capt. R. P. Johnson on the north side of the Savannah River in South Carolina and was buried with military honors.

18. 1815 — Mary Ann Tudor — Miss Tudor came to Savannah on a ship from Barbados. The cause of her death after she arrived here was listed as Sea Sickness. Her brother had her body placed in a keg of rum and transported back to Barbados for burial there.

19. 1818 — Richard Kimball — The young man buried beneath this stone ornamented with a classic urn and drapery is typical of a number of young men who came South for their health. He came to Savannah from Connecticut, ill with consumption. He hoped the warmer climate would enable him to recover his health.

20. 1818 — John S. Ally — Mr. Ally was a merchant tailor who died at the age of 51 by drinking cold water when heated.

21. 1849 — James Poince — Poince died as the result of the accidental discharge of a gun. He was on board a

ship in the harbor at the time, and the gun was in the hands of a friend.

22. 1824 — Major Hugh McCall — McCall was born in North Carolina. He was a Brevet Major in the United States Army. He wrote the first history of Georgia, the first volume of which was published in 1811, and the second, in 1816.

23. 1826 — Charles Perony DeIstria — He was born in Corsica, and earned his living as a fencing master. The cause of his death was ironically noted in the death register as a "casualty."

CAPTAIN JOHN DARTHIAGUE

No stone stands in Colonial Cemetery to mark the grave of Captain John Darthiague, a sea captain who committed suicide. Perhaps the grave was never marked, but it is more likely that the marker has gone the way of so many other missing markers. Only a notice that appeared on January 19, 1786, in the *Gazette of the State of Georgia*, states that Capt. Darthiague lies buried here.

According to the article that appeared in the newspaper, the following event took place on January 15, 1786:

> On Sunday the 1st instant, at half after six o'clock in the morning, Capt. John Darthiague, of this place shot himself in the head with two pistols to the great astonishment, regret, and concern of his numerous friends and acquaintances. He lingered till Wednesday night the 11th when he died. Next day a Jury of Inquest sat on his body and brought in their verdict, Insanity, at the time he committed the act. In the evening his remains were attended to the Burying Ground by a number of respectable citizens and strangers and decently interred.

MARY CAHILL

Near the back gate on Perry Lane, to the left of the tabby path, is a simple stone. It marks the grave of William Cahill, a native of Ireland, age thirty-nine, who died October 21, 1802. He was a cooper by trade. An infant daughter, Mary, aged fourteen days, is also buried here. William's wife Mary, also a native of Ireland, was left a widow with two small children. According to legal notices which were published in the newspapers of the day, William had some property which Mary inherited. A Mr. John Trevor was named administrator of William's affairs.

Perhaps Mary never was able to cope with the death of her husband, or perhaps other problems arose which were too much for her to handle. Whatever the reasons, Mary Cahill took her own life November 17, 1803, by cutting her throat. She was survived by two small children who apparently were to inherit some property. Mr. John Trevor of Savannah was also named as the administrator of Mary's affairs. A notice of sale in the *Georgia Republican and State Intelligencer,* dated January 13, 1804, lists "the property and effects of Mrs. Mary Cahill, deceased, consisting of SHOP, GOODS, AND HOUSEHOLD FURNITURE".

The final chapter to this tragic family occurred January 28, 1804, when it was recorded in the *Register of Deaths in Savannah* that Ann Cahill, age four years, daughter of William and Mary Cahill, died of croup. Of the surviving son of William and Mary, there is no further mention.

While I do not care to speculate on the events that occurred, it is obvious that there is no marker for Mary Cahill in Colonial Cemetery. Although her grave site is unknown, it is highly likely that she is buried nearby, if not with her husband and child.

ALTERED INSCRIPTIONS

The following list reflects the alterations made to some of the grave stones by Union troops during their occupation of Savannah. Some of the changes are rather crudely done, while others show some degree of expertise.

1. Josiah Muir, Aged 11 and wife Mary, age 17 and son Lewis Phoenix, aged 12 years
Location: Mounted on the east wall.
2. Onesime Legriel, age 138 yrs., Nerestan Legriel, age 139 yrs., Charles P. DeIstria, age 620 yrs.
Location: This large slab is to the left of the walk at Abercorn St. gate, near fence.
3. Susannah Gray, age 121 yrs. and 1124 days
Location: On the west side near the fence on Abercorn, to the right of Abercorn gate.
4. Patrick Stanton, age 183 yrs
Location: The west side, a large slab, near Abercorn St.
5. Ursula Herb, born 1711— died 1811— age 73 yrs. & 12 days (Index of deaths: d. 1814, age 84). Thus, her birth date is 1730/1741; probably, 1741 is correct birth date.
Location: To the right of the walk from Abercorn-Oglethorpe corner gate., age 129 yrs.
6. Thomas M. Cooper
Location: To the left of walk from front entrance — behind brick vaults.

The stone of Josiah Muir. Both Josiah, and his son
Lewis Phoenix Muir, were yellow fever victims. This
stone is obviously one of the many stones altered by
Union soldiers.

7. Capt. Jonathan Cooper, age 1700 yrs.

Location: Same as above.

8. Julia Ann Cooper, age 425 yrs.

Location: Same as above.

9. Catherine Morecock, age 69 — Phillip D. Woolhopter,
age 1491, and infant children, Sarah Ann Woolhopter,
age 10 mos., 1271 days. — also a sketch of what looks like
Ft. Pulaski at bottom of slab.

Location: This is a large slab on left side of walk that
turns east from main gate.

10. Caroline J. Lloyd, age 1171 yrs.

Location: Between the Hunter vault and the Bolton plot.

11. Maurice Cody. aged 146 yrs.

Location: Near the end of the path leading to the southwest corner.

12. Anne Watts, aged 125 yrs.

 Location: Behind the Gwinnett memorial.

13. William Davies Berrien, 627th yr of his age.

Location: In the cluster of box tombs near the Tiot vault.

14. W. Richardson, Sr., aged 155 years.

Location: Near the front entrance, between the Hunter vault and the Bolton plot.

15. William Neyle. Aged 341 years.

Location: To the right of the entrance near the Anne Guerard tomb.

16. Mrs. Ann McLaughlin. Aged 186 years.

Location: Next to Anne Guerard.

17. Mrs. M. E. Long. Age 162 years.

Location: Next to Anne Guerard.

18. Edward Ellington. Age 152 years.

Location: The middle slab to the left of the entrance.

19. Mrs. Rachel Wier. Aged 153.

Location: Behind the Thompson vault and to the right of the Schick vault.

20. Miss Caroline Elizabeth Jacqueline deRossignol Belleanse. Born Nov. 4, 1807-Died January 8, 1807, aged 31years.

Location: On west side, near fence on Abercorn Street close to Abercorn Street gate.

21. Christopher McDonald, aged 421 years.

Location: Mounted on the east wall.

GENEALOGICAL DATA

The stones in Colonial Cemetery contain a wealth of information on the persons buried there. The maiden names of women, as well as their parents' names, are frequently given. A person's birth order is also sometimes included. This was a way of connecting the person to a family and establishing the person's place within the family.

The following genealogical data has been carefully abstracted from a number of various sources. These sources include the stones themselves, *Some Early Epitaphs in Georgia,* the *Annals of Georgia Mortuary Records,* newspaper obituaries, and the *Death Registers for Savannah.* Where discrepancies in names or dates were noted in comparing the sources, I selected the name or date which either appeared on the stone, or which seemed to be the most accurate interpretation based on the amount of available information.

Some of the names listed here do not have matching monuments in Colonial Cemetery. However, available information indicates that they were buried here, and in many cases, they are buried with or near other family members. Many of the monuments and stones have long since disappeared. Those which remain are often illegible. When possible, I attempted to compare the written records with the stones themselves. Errors frequently occurred in both the *Annals of Georgia* and also in *Some Early Epitaphs.* Some of these were obviously transcription errors. Others were errors of omission. I tried to correct those which I knew to be in error in order to assure the researcher of as much accurate information as was possible.

Colonial Park Cemetery, Savannah, GA

Abbott, Wesley. Native of NJ; b. ca. 1798; d. 31 Oct. 1842; age 44 yrs. Resident of Savannah last 16 yrs.

Alexander, Mrs. Louisa. Born in Stuttgardt, Germany; b. 23 Mar. 1777; d. 1 Oct. 1846; age 69 yrs.; wid./o Dr. Adam Alexander.

Anderson, Mrs.D. b. ca. 1742; d. 5 May 1812; age 70 yrs. (in Wallace lot).

Andrew, Mary Overton. b. ca. Jan. 1819; d. 27 Sept. 1822; age 3 yrs. 8 mos.; 2nd d/o Rev. James O. Andrew.

Anthony, Albert. b. ca. 1856; d. 18 May 1858; age 2 yrs.

Armstrong, Jane. b. ca. 1774; d. 18 Oct. 1806; age 32 yrs.

Arnold, Amie. d. 1872; age 78 yrs. Believed to be a misplaced stone. No records found.

Ash. James Barrows. age 7 wks.

Ash, John H. b. ca. 14 Feb. 1793; d. 4 Sept. 1822; age 29 yrs. 7 mos. 21 dys.

Ash, Mary Catherine. age 18 mos.

Ash, Sarah Harris. b. ca. 25 Feb. 1821; d. 13 Mar. 1834; age 13 yrs. 1 mo. 17 dys.; d/o John E. & Sarah Ash.

Ash, Sarah. b. ca. 1791; d. 18 June 1836.

Ash, Theodora. b. ca. 1753; d. 17 Feb. 1770; age 17.

Atherton, John. b. 1769; d. Sept. 1824; age 55 yrs.

Atkinson, Isaiah. b. 1788; d. 2 Sept. 1823; left wife.

Atkinson, Margaret. b. ca. 1791; d. 28 Dec. 1812; age 21; w/o George Atkinson.

Atkinson, Susan. b. ca. 1771; d. 6 May 1808; age 37; w/o George Atkinson.

Bain, Sarah A. b. 1805; d. 7 Mar. 1830; age 25 yrs.

Baker, Job F. Native of NJ; b. ca. 27 May 1785; d. 1 July 1818; age 1 mo. 8 dys.

Baldwin, Amelia Caroline. b. 1 Feb. 1805; d. 10 Feb. 1843; age 38 yrs. w/o L. Baldwin.

Baldwin, Eliza Caroline. b. 15 Dec. 1831; d. 22 Dec. 1834; age 3 yrs.; d/o Loami & Amelia C. Baldwin.

Baldwin, Loami. Born Shrewsbury, MA; b. 1 Aug. 1786; d. 27 Sept. 1847; age 61 yrs. h/o Amelia Caroline Baldwin; Died in Boston, MA.

Baldwin, William Henry. b. 5 Sept. 1825; d. 30 Oct. 1830; age 5 yrs.; s/o Loami & Amelia Caroline Baldwin.

Ball, Frederick. b. ca. 1801; d. 18 Aug. 1820; age 19 yrs. Yellow Fever.

Ballantine, John. Born in Scotland; b. 12 Nov. 1794; d. 22 Oct. 1838.

Barrie, James. Native of Monedie Parish, Perthshire, North Britain; b. 1785; d. 10 Oct. 1817; age 32 yrs.

Batty, George. Of Providence, R.I.; b. ca. 1777; d. 20 Sept. 1814; age 37; left widow and children.

Bayard, Mary Ann. b. 6 Feb. 1813; d. 9 Apr. 1850; w/o William H. McIntosh; d/o George ?Bayard & Catherine McIntosh.

Bayard, Nicholas, M.D. b. ca. 1774; d. 30 Oct. 1821; age 47 yrs.

Bayley, Mary F. b. ca. 1806; d. 10 Nov. 1817; age 11 yrs.; adopted d/o William M. & Sophia Evans of Savannah.

Beasley, Mary E. b. ca.31 July 1836; d. 16 Nov. 1838; age 2 yrs. 3 mos. 16 dys.; d/o Joshua & Susan A. Beasley.

Beaulard, John A. Born in Paris, France; b. 1788; d. 15 Mar. 1836; h/o Eugenia J. Beaulard.

Belcher, Grace Carr. b. 1748; d. 14 Jan. 1793; age 45 yrs.; w/o Mr. James Belcher.

Belcher, James Pryce. b. Apr.1788; d. 21 Feb. 1793; age 4 yrs. 10 mos.; s/o Mrs. Grace Carr Belcher.

Belcher, John C. d. 23 Nov. 1794; s/o William & Eleanor Belcher of Savannah.

Belcher, William Dickinson. d. 6 June 1803; s/o William & Eleanor Belcher of Savannah.

Belleanse, Caroline Elizabeth Jacqueline DeRossignol. b.4 Nov. 1807. Gowvaines, Hispaniola; d. 9 Jan. 1838.

Bennett, Susan Elizabeth. b. ca. 23 July 1817; d. 16 Dec. 1835; age 8 yrs. 4 mos. 24 dys.; d/o Amasa & Abbey Adeline Bennett.

Benning, Elizabeth C. b. 1807; d. 17 Jan. 1834; age 27 yrs.; w/o Thomas C. Benning.

Bentley, Elizabeth. b. ca. 1772; d. 7 Aug. 1827; age 55; w/o John Bentley of Savannah, Ga.

Berrien Elizabeth. d. 27 Aug. 1828; w/o John MacPherson Berrien; only d/o Nicholas & Lydia Anciaux; died in Greenville, SC.

Berrien, Maj. John. b. ca. 1759; d. 6 Nov. 1815.

Berrien, Nicholas Anciaux. b. 22 June 1816; d. 17 June 1817; fourth s/o John MacPherson Berrien & Eliza, his wife.

Berrien, Richard M., M.D. b. ca. 1795; d. 20 Sept. 1820; age 25 yrs. Yellow fever.

Berrien, William Davis. b. ca. 1813; d. 2 Dec. 1840 at Ft. Brooke, East FL; 1st Lt. 6th Reg. U.S. Inf.

Betts, George. Native of Hudson, NY; b. 1809; d. 3 Feb. 1845; age 36 yrs.; resident of Savannah for last 14 yrs.

Bevan, Joseph Vallance. Born in Liberty Co., GA; b. 1798; d. 29 Mar. 1830; age 32 yrs.

Bills, Margaret S. b. 1819; d. 19 Oct. 1840; age 21 yrs. Also infant babe.

Bird, William. Native of Co. Tyrone, Ireland; b. 1796; d. 4 Aug. 1824; age 28 yrs.

Blackmar, Francis Burton. Native of Savannah; d. 1 June 1829; s/o Alfred O. & Elizabeth B. Blackmar.

Blaine, Ephraim M., M.D. Of Carlisle, PA; d. 13 Mar. 183—; age 39 yrs.; Asst. Surgeon, U.S. Army; had a sis.

Blancho, Ann. Native of Georgia; b. 1820; d. 20 Dec. 1827; age 27 yrs.

Blois, Margaret Adel. b. ca. 9 May; 1807; d. 19 Oct. 1817; age 10 yrs. 5 mos. 11 dys.

Bogert, John. b. ca. 19 Nov.1784; d. 20 June 1804; age 19 yrs. 9 mos. 1 dy. s/o Nicholas Bogert of New York.

Boggs, Joseph M., M.D. b. ca. 24 May 1831; d. 24 Aug. 1852; age 21 yrs. 3 mos.

Bolan, Mrs. Sarah H. b. 1803; d. 20 Dec. 1842; age 39 yrs.; w/o James Bolan, Esq. of SC.

Bolles, Gustavus A. Native of CT. b.1777; d. 17 Oct. 1819; age 42 yrs.

Bolton, Robert. b. 1722; d. 1789.

Bolton, Robert, Jr. of Savannah; b. ca. 1 Dec. 1757; d. 4 Dec. 1802; age 45 yrs. 3 dys.; Merchant.

Borde, Peter E. Born in Martinique; b. ca. 1801; d. 12 Sept. 1822; age 21 yrs.

Boulineau, Edward Augustus. b. ca. 183—; d. 6 May 183—; age 15 mos. 7 dys.; s/o Augustus & Mary Ann Boulineau.

Bowen, Elizabeth. Born in SC; b. ca. 1745; d. 12 Nov. 1808.

Bowman, George Freeland. b. 10 Dec. 1831; d. 15 Sept. 1836; s/o Charles & Hannah L. Bowman.

Boynton, Mrs. Betsy. Native of Gerry, N.S. b. ca. 1781; d. 4 Nov. 1820; age 39.

Bradley, Noah W. Native of Greenfield, CT.; b. Feb. 1776; d. 1811.

Brooks, Benjamin. Native of Norwalk, CT.; b. ca. 1794; d. 23 Mar. 1817; age 44. Resident of Savannah for many years.

Brown, George. Native of Edinburgh, Scotland; b. 1780; d. 23 Dec. 1833.

Brown, John. Born in Ireland. b. ca. 1796; d. 22 Oct. 1826.

Brown, John H. Of Richmond, Va.; b. 22 Oct.1778, Mecklenburg Co., Va.; d.1811, Savannah, Ga.; left a widow.

Brown, Joseph. b. 18 Aug. 1922; d. 7 Feb. 1944; Pvt. Air Corps; Georgia.

Brown, Mary. Native of Hollistown, MA.; b. ca. 1794; d. 23 Oct. 1819; age 25; w/o David Brown.

Brown, Mary Ann W. b. ca. 27 Mar. 1818; d. 8 June 1819; age 1 yr. 2 mo. & 13 dys.; only child of David & Mary Brown.

Bruen, Anna Matilda. b. ca. 17 June 1819; d. 13 July 1825; age 6 yrs. 26 dys.; d/o Wickliffe & Matilda Bruen.

Bruen, George Knox. b. ca. 31 Aug. 1839; d. 4 Sept. 1839; age 5 dys. s/o Wickliffe & Matilda Bruen.

Bryan, Charles W. b. 24 May 1829; d. 11 Feb. 18—; s/o Rev. Samuel V. & Elizabeth J. Bryan.

Bryan, Henry B. b. 1 Aug. 1818; d. 1 Aug. 1818; inf.s/o Rev. Samuel V. & Elizabeth J. Bryan.

Bryan, Mary. b. ca. 1702; d. 26 May 1766; age 64 yrs.; wid./o Joseph Bryan of SC.

Bryan, Mary C. b. 28 Dec. 1816; d. 18 Mar. 1817; inf. d/o Rev. Samuel V. & Elizabeth J. Bryan.

Bryan, Samuel K. b 17 Dec. 1820; d. 12 May 1821; inf.s/o Rev. Samuel V. & Elizabeth J. Bryan.

Bulloch, Archibald. Native of S.C. b. 1730 in SC; d. 1777; 1st Pres. of Ga. Patriot & soldier.

Bunch, Samuel Green. Native of New Providence, Nassau.; b. 1776; d. 16 Nov. 1816; age 40 yrs.

Burk, Mrs.Henrietta. No dates; w/o Hewett D. Burk.

Burroughs, Benjamin. b. ca. 1 Apr. 1780; d. 14 Apr. 1837; age. 57 yrs. 14 dys.

Butler, James. Born in England; b. ca. 1807; d. 31 Oct. 1817.

Butler, James M. b. 12 Oct. 1835; d. 3 Nov. 1837; s/o James M. & Mary E. Butler.

Cahill, Ann. b. ca. 1800; d. Jan. 1804; age 4 yrs.; d/o William & Mary Cahill.

Cahill, Mary. Born in Ireland; b. ca. 1773; d. 17 Nov. 1803; age 30 yrs.; w/o William Cahill; left young son & dau.; suicide?

Cahill, Mary. inf. d/o William & Mary Cahill; age 14 dys.

Cahill, William. b. 1763; d. 21 Oct. 1802; age 39 yrs.; h/o Mary Cahill.

Campfield, Ann Marian. b. ca. 2 Dec.1827; d. 22 May 1829; age 1 yr. 6 mos. 20 dys.; d/o Nathaniel & Lydia Campfield.

Carnochan, Harriott Margaret. b. 27 Feb. 1812; d. 8 June 1812.

Carnochan, Jane M. age 7 yrs. 3 mos.

Carnochan, Susan Rebecca. b. 11 Sept. 1807; d. 16 May 1808.

Carter, Rev. Abiel, A.M. b. 2 Mar. 1791 in Concord, NH.; d. 15 Nov. 1827; h/o Maria Beach; Rector of Christ Church, Savannah.

Carter, Maria Beach. b. 8 Aug. 1791; 28 Oct. 1827; d/o Abraham Beach, D.D., late of New Brunswick, NJ.

Casey, William. Native of Parish Ballingarry, Co. Limerick, Ireland; b. 1787; d. 8 Aug. 1836; age 49 yrs.

Castoff, Jeremiah. Of Newport, RI; d. 2 July 1820; Yellow Fever.

Catonnet, Mrs. Ann. Born in Georgia; b. 1778; d. 23 Mar. 1830; age 52 yrs.; w/o Peter Catonnet.

Cavanagh, James. Born in Co. Kildare, Ireland; 1794; d. 13 Oct. 1818; age 24 yrs.

Chadbourn, Isabella. b. ca. 14 Dec. 1828; d. 19 June 1850; age 21 yrs. 7 mos. 5 dys.; w/o Jacob Chadbourn.

Charlton, Ann. Native of England; d. 1 Aug. 18—0; age 25 yrs.; w/o Robert Charlton; had chdn.

Chevrier, Dr. Jean Baptiste. Born in Paris, France; b. 10 July 1787; d. 10 Dec. 1839.

Christie, Lawrence. Born in NJ; b. ca. 1781; d. 16 Nov. 1826.

Christie, Robert. b. ca. 1787; d. 24 Dec. 1822; age 35 yrs.

Christy, Mrs. Victoria (Veronica). Native of Saint Domingue; resident of Savannah last 17 yrs.; b. ca, 1769; d. 22 July 1827.

Claghorn, P.P. b. ca. 1792; d. 4 July 1844; age 52 yrs.

Claghorn, R.S. b. ca. 1815; d. 31 Oct. 1838; age 23 yrs.

Claghorn, Samuel. b. ca. 1787; d. 22 Oct. 1840; age 53 yrs.

Clark, Andrew. b.1791; d. 28 July 1820; age 29 yrs.

Clark, Anna. Born in New Orleans, LA; b. 1842; d. 8 May 1844; brought dead from New Orleans.

Clark, Howard. b. ca. 1811; d. 25 Sept. 1811; age 15 mos.; s/o Joseph & Mary Clark.

Clark, James A. Native of New York; b. 1800; d. 7 Oct. 1826; age 26 yrs.

Clark, Joanna. b. 1761; d. 27 Nov. 1808; age 47 yrs.; w/o James Clark.

Clark, Lawrence Ludlow. b. ca. Nov. 1813; d. 15 May 1815; age 19 mos.; s/o Joseph & Mary Clark.

Clay, Ann. b. ca. 1743; d. 1 Dec. 1821; age 78 yrs.

Clay, Joseph. Born in England; b. 16 Oct.1741; d. 15 Nov. 1804.

Cleland, James. Native of Ireland; b. ca. 1757; d. 20 July 1818; age 61 yrs.

Cleland, Moses. Native of Ireland; b. ca. 1767; d. 18 Aug. 1832; age 65 yrs.

Cleland, William. Native of Ireland; b. ca. 1772; d. 11 Oct. 1804; age 32 yrs.

Cler, Frederick. b. ca. 12 July 1829; d. 30 July 1851; age 22 yrs. 18 dys.

Clifford, Charles Goodrich. b. ca. 29 Oct. 1839; d. 13 Nov. 1840; age 1 yr. 15 dys.; s/o James A. & Jane Clifford.

Clizbe, Isaac Watts. Native of Newark, NJ. b. ca. 14 Apr. 1792; d. 29 Dec. 1817; age 25 yrs. 8 mos. 15 dys.

Clizby, Samuel. b. ca. Jan. 1783; d. 3 Oct. 1819; age 35 yrs. 10 mos.

Coburn, Mary Ann. Born in Providence, RI; b. 19 Jan. 1806; d. 27 Aug. 1841; age 35 yrs. 7 mos. 8 dys.; w/o Moses Coburn; d/o Capt. Peter & Rebecca Douville.

Coburn, Mary Ann. Born in Savannah; b. 1831; d. 25 Sept. 1834; d/o Moses & Mary Ann Coburn

Cody, Maurice. Native of Co. Cork, Ireland; b. 1787; d. 6 Feb. 1833; age 46 yrs. Left a nephew.

Coe, George W. b. ca. 1790; d. 22 Sept. 1832; age 42 yrs.

Coe, William. Born at Springfield, NJ. b. 22 Dec. 1795; d. 4 Sept. 1830; age 35 yrs. 8 mos.

Coffin, Anna Mary. b. ca. 28 Dec. 1820; d. 13 Mar. 1821; age 4 mos. 16 dys.; only d/o Francis & Louisa M. Coffin.

Cole, Francis B. b. ca. 7 Oct. 1845; d. 31 Dec. 1848; age 3 yrs. 2 mos. 23 dys.; only s/o F. T. & J. E. Cole.

Coleman, Infant. d. Jan. 1812; child of J. A. & Eleanor Coleman.

Coleman, J. A. d. 1817.

Coleman, Eleanor. d. 1817

Cole, Margaret E. b. ca. 3 Nov. 1843; d. 14 Dec. 1848; age 5 yrs. 2 mos. 25 dys.; d/o F.T. & J. E. Cole.

Coleman, Robert. b. ca. 11 Aug. 1806; d. 25 May 1814; age 7 yrs. 11 mos. 14 dys.; s/o J. A. & Eleanor Coleman.

Collins, Margaret. b. ca. 1 May 1836; d. 13 Aug. 1848; age 12 yrs. 5 mos. 13 dys; d/o Timothy & Julia Collins; died at House of Sisters of Mercy in Savannah.

Condy, Thomas Hollis, Jr. d. 1821.

Conlin, Patrick. Native of Parish of Athboy, Co. Meath, Ireland. b. 1775; d. 9 Feb. 1817; age 42 yrs.

Connerat, Catherine. Native of Mole St. Nicholas, Island of St. Domingue; b. 1789; d. 21 May 1839; age 50 yrs.

Connerat, Francis. Native of Mole St. Nicholas, Island of St. Domingue; b. 1777; d. 14 May 1823; age 46 yrs.; left a wife.

Connelly, Patrick. Native of Killesshandin, Co. Cavan, Ireland; b. 1791; d. 25 Aug. 1826; age 35 yrs.; left wid.

Connolly, Maryan. Native of Thurles, Co. Tipperary, Ireland; b. 1808; d. 2 Sept. 1827; age 19 yrs.

Conway, Robert Emmett. b. ca. 1 Apr. 1842; d. 1 June 1842; age 1 mo. 28 dys.; s/o Martin & Margaret L. Conway.

Cooke, Henry P. Native of New York City; b. ca. Feb. 1807; d. 4 Oct. 1838; lived in Savannah for the last nine years.

Cooper, Ann Caroline. b. ca. July 1818; d. 1 Sept. 1828; age 10 yrs. 2 mos. d/o Ephrium & Lidia Cooper.

Cooper, Capt. Jonathan. Born in Wexford, Ireland; b. ca. 1768; d. 13 Mar. 1838; age 70 yrs.

Cooper, Julia Ann. b. ca. 1794; d. 23 Nov. 1819; age 25 yrs.; w/o Capt. J. Cooper.

Cooper, Sarah Jane. Native of Baltimore, MD. b. ca. 1817; d. 26 Aug. 1839; age 22 yrs. w/o Peter G. Cooper; resident of Savannah since infancy.

Cooper, Thomas M. b. ca. Aug. 1809; d. 12 Feb. 1839; age 29 yrs. 6 mos.

Cooper, William. age 1 yr. 6 mos; s/o Capt. J. & Julia Ann Cooper.

Cornell, Clementine C. d. 3 June 1838.

Cornell, John J. d. 20 Sept. 1849.

Cornick, John L. Native of Bridgeport, England; b. ca. 1797; d. 14 Nov. 1827; age 30 yrs.

Cottineau, Achilles J. M De Kerloguen. b. ca. 1790; d. 11 July 1812; age 22 yrs. s/o Denis L.Cottineau Aude Kerloguen.

Cottineau, Denis L. Aude Kerloguen. Native of Nantes, France; b. 1745; d. 29 Nov. 1808; age 63 yrs.; member of The Cincinnati Society.

Cotton, James W. Native of New York; b. ca. 1792; d. 26 Sept. 1820; age 28 years.

Cowper, Mary. b. ca. 1752; d. 10 Apr. 1821; age 69 yrs.; d/o John & Elizabeth Smith; wid./o Basil Cowper.

Craig, Edward William. b. ca. 22 Apr. 1823; d. 18 May 1823; age 27 dys.; s/o William M. & Lucy A. Craig.

Craig, William, A. B. Born at Rumney, NH; b. 1768; d. 27 Aug. 1821; age 53 yrs.

Craven, Richard E. W. b. ca. 25 Jan. 1825; d. 19 July 1842; age 17 yrs. 6 mos. 25 dys.; s/o Richard N. Craven.

Crews, Miss Lydia A. b. 1821; d. 13 Apr. 1848; age 21 yrs.

Croker, Mrs. Eliza. Native of Amelia Island, East Florida; b. 1817; d. 3 July 1840; age 23 yrs.; also her inf. babe.

Cummings, John. d. 2 Sept. 1835. Died in Newport, RI.

Cummins, John. Native of Kildare, Ireland; b. ca. 1778; d. 11 Oct. 1809; age 31 yrs.; left wid. & chdn.

Currie, Alexander. b. ca. 1775; d. 12 Feb. 1813; age 38. bro./o John Currie, Esq.

Currie, John, Esq. Native of Galloway, Scotland; b. ca. 1762; d. 27 Sept. 1799; age 37 yrs. bro./o Alexander Currie.

Cushman, Ezra. Native of New Bedford, MA; b. 1772; d. 13 Sept. 1802; age 30 yrs.; left wid.

Cuthbert, George, Esq. d. 14 Apr. 1768.

Cuyler, Telemon. b. 1730; d. 29 Sept. 1772; age 42 yrs.

Daily, Edward. d. 26 Nov. 1832; s/o John & Frances Daily.

Daily, Frances. d. 23 Mar. 1850; w/o John Daily; m/o Edward Daily.

Danforth, George. Native of Schoharie Co., NY; b.1789; d. 16 Aug. 1831; age 42 yrs. Attorney at Law; had wife & chdn.

Davidson, Mr. John. Of East Haven, CT; b. 1778; d. 3 Sept. 1817; age 39 yrs.

Davies, Charles. Native of Ireland; resident of New York 20 yrs.; b. ca. 1793; d. 11 Oct. 1817; age 34 yrs. Had a sister.

Dawson, A. L. b. 1841; d. 5 Oct. 1847; age 6 yrs.; s/o Richard & Ann Dawson.

Dawson, Richard. Native of SC; d. 19 May 1835.

Dawson, Samuel. d. 2 Oct. 1838; s/o Samuel & Sarah Dawson.

Dayton, Sarah Antoinette. b. 1819; d. 9 Oct. 1821; age 2 yrs.

De Istria, Charles Perony. Born at Ajacio, Island of Corsica; b. 6 Aug. 1764; d. 13 Jan. 1826; age 62 yrs. 5 mos.; fencing master; casualty.

DeLamassee, Paul P. Thomasson. Born at Castillon Dept. de la Gironde, France; b. 23 Apr.1776; d. 12 Jan. 1834; Consul of France; had wife & chdn.; died in Savannah.

Delberghe, Mrs. Elizabeth. b. 1793; d. 9 Nov. 1816; age 23 yrs.; w/o John Delberghe; d/o Francis Roma of Savannah; left a dau. & a sis.

Delberghe, John. Native of the Netherlands; b. ca. Nov. 1778; d. 10 July 1829; age 50 yrs. 9 mos.; h/o Elizabeth Roma Delberghe.; resident of Savannah 25 yrs.

Delony, Mrs. Martha. b. ca. 1765; d.18 Sept. 1820. wid./o William Delony, Esq.; Yellow Fever.

Demera, Mary Elizabeth. b. ca. 1759; d. 31 Oct. 1783; age 24 yrs.

Dempster, James. Native of Cooper in Fife, Scotland; b. 1760; d. 18 Oct. 1802; age 42 yrs. Left a wid.

Denmark, Mary. b. 1795; d. 18 Feb. 1814; w/o Allen Denmark.

Dennison, Ann Maria. age 1 yr. 10 mos.; d/o Lewis W. Dennison.

Dennison, Lewis W. Native of Dantzick, Prussia; b. ca. Feb. 1802; d. 17 Sept. 1830; age 28 yrs. 7 mos.

De Segur, Heloisa Georgiana. b. ca. Mar. 1824; d. 5 Oct. 1827; age 3 yrs. 7 mos.; d/o Joseph F. & Celia De Segur.

De Segur, Joseph Henry. b. ca. Aug. 1825; d. 25 Oct. 1828; age 3 yrs. 2 mos.; s/o Joseph F. & Celia De Segur.

Desmond, Dennis. Native of Parish of Ballinora County, Ireland; b. 1783; d. 4 July 1818; age 35 yrs.; h/o of Catherine Mann Desmond.

D'Espinose, Jerome Francois. Native of St. Domingue; b. 1746; d. 16 June 1810; age 64 yrs.; left wife, Clair Adelaide Armaignac D'Espinose.

Devillers, Francois Didier Petit. b. Villers La Montagni, Mozelle, France; b. 10 Jan. 1761; d. 8 May 1841.

Dickinson, Capt. Jeremiah. b. 1740; d. 21 Dec. 1797; age 57 yrs.; drowned in rescue attempt.

Dickson, John. Born in England; b. ca. 1789; d. 1818; age 29 yrs.

Dillon, John. Native of Killcock, Co. Kildare, Ireland; b. 1797; d. 13 May 1831; age 34 yrs.; left a bro.

Dillon, Mary Ann. b. ca. Jan. 1823; d. 5 Oct. 1825; age 1 yr. 9 mos.

Doon, Mr. John Glascock. Native of Ballyrom, Queen's County, Ireland; b. 1774; d. 8 Jan. 1814; age 40 yrs.; left widow & chdn.

Dorsett, John, Sr., b, city of New York, Oct. 1813; d. Savannah 5 Oct. 1846; f/o John, Jr., and Sarah R. Dorsett, Sarah R.; b. 15 Apr. 1841; d. 1 Mar. 1842

Dorsett, Rhoda Watts. b. ca. 19 Nov. 1807; d. 25 Apr. 1840; age 32 yrs. 6 mos. 6 dys.; d/o Joseph & Martha Dorsett.

Doty, Jane Cornelia. b. ca. Dec. 1843; d. 2 Feb. 1845; age 14 mos.; d/o Morris & Catherine Doty.

Dow, Amos. b. ca. Mar, 1787; d. 28 Sept. 1820; age 33 yrs. 6 mos.; Yellow Fever.

Driscoll, Capt. Lawrence C. Native of Ireland; b. 1763; d. 21 Apr. 1810; age 47 yrs.; h/o Margaret Driscoll.

Drouillard, Andrew. Born in France; b. 25 July 1758; d. 11 Feb. 1825; left companion of 36 yrs. Had chdn. Inhabitant of Chatham Co. GA for 28 yrs.; died on his plantation near Savannah.

Drysdale, Ann. d. 1 Nov. 1820; w/o John Drysdale.

Drysdale, Ann Johnston. b. 1809; d. 10 Mar. 1819; age 10 yrs.; d/o John & Ann Drysdale.

Duebeel, John Henry. Native of Elpenroth, Germany. b. ca. 1766; d. 1 July 1815; age 49.

Dunigan, Patrick. Born in Ireland; b. ca. 1783; d. 1 Oct. 1819; age 36 yrs.

Dunn,————. Born in Lincolnshire, England; b. ca. 1759; d. 10 Oct. 1815; age 56 yrs.

Dunn, James. Native of New Jersey. Respectable resident of Savannah.

Eagerty, John. Native of Co. Kerry, Ireland; b. 1819; d. 5 Dec. 1845; age 26 yrs.; bro./o Thomas & Michael Eagerty.

Eagerty, Michael. Native of Co. Kerry, Ireland; b. 1803; d. 3 May 1846; age 43 yrs.; bro./o Thomas & John Eagerty.

Eastmaid, George J. b. ca. 10 Dec. 1836; d. 29 Aug. 1838; age 1 yr. 9 mos. 19 dys.

Eastmaid, Virginia E. b. ca. 16 Dec. 1832; d. 9 Aug. 1836; age 3 yrs. 9 mos. 25 dys.

Eaton, Theodosius. b. 1784; d. 29 May 1835 (or 2 June 1835); age 51 yrs.; m/o Timothy Eaton of Boston, MA.

Elbert, Elizabeth Rae. d. 26 Jan. 1792 at Great Ogeechee, GA; wid./o Samuel Elbert; d/o John Rae. Had 6 chdn.

Elbert, Samuel. Born St. Williams Parish, SC; b. ca. 1740; d. ca. 6 Nov. 1788; interred in Colonial Cemetery 11 Mar. 1927; s/o William & Sarah Elbert who came to SC from England in 1732; m. Elizabeth Rae 1769.

Ellington, Edward. Native of England; b. ca. 1720; d. 30 Oct. 1795; age 75 yrs.; in America 28 yrs.; Rector of Christ Church.

Elon, Jane. b. ca. 1801; d. 20 Sept. 1820; age 19; Yellow Fever.

Elon, William. b. 1792; d. 15 Sept. 1820; age 28 yrs.; Yellow Fever.

England, Jane. b. ca. Sept. 1798; d. 26 Dec. 1848; age 50 yrs. 3 mos.; midwife.

Erich, George. Late of New York; b. 1802; d. 29 Dec. 1816; age 14 yrs.

Ernaut, Francis. Born in France. b. ca. 1770.

Evans, Mr. John J. d. Jan. 1813.

Evans, Margaret Evritt. b. 1808; d. 15 Aug. 1812; age 4 yrs.

Evans, Sarah. age 67 yrs.

Evans, William. b. 1785; d. 22 Apr. 1820; age 32 yrs.

Fair, Robert. Born Cavon Co., Ireland. b.1769; d. 18 Dec. 1820; age 52 yrs.

Fannin, Abraham Baldwin. d. bef. 1822; s/o A. B.& Jane Fannin.

Fannin, Mrs. Jane. b. 15 Oct. 1804; m. 15 Nov. 1822; d. 27 Aug. 1835; w/o A. B. Fannin; had 8 chdn.; 4 preceded her in death.

Fannin, Mary Thomas. d. bef. 1835; d/o A. B. & Jane Fannin.

Fannin, Elizabeth Saffold.   d. bef. 1835; buried at Brampton, near Savannah; d/o A. B. & Jane Fannin.

Fannin, Virginia. d. bef. 1835; bur. Milledgeville, GA; d/o A. B. & Jane Fannin.

Farley, Sarah. b. ca. 1785/1725; d. 5 Apr. 1812; age 37/87 yrs.

Farmer, Asael. Born in NC; b. ca. 1743; d. 30 Mar. 1811/ age 68 yrs.

Feldt, William H. d. Aug. 1818.

Fell, Frederick S. b. 1788; d. 9 Nov. 1831; age 43 yrs.; prop. & editor *Savannah Republican*.

Fell, Harriot H. b. ca. 1792; d. 9 Oct. 1826; age 34 yrs.

Fell, Isaac. Born in Lancaster, England; came to Savannah 1782; cabinet maker.

Fenton, Mary. Native of New Jersey; b. 1780; d. 11 Oct. 1814; age 34 yrs.

Ferguson, Mrs. Mary. Native of Savannah; b. 1767; d. 22 Oct. 1816; age 49 yrs.

Field, Mrs. Agnes G. b. ca. Jan. 1796; d. 18 Mar. 1836; age 46 yrs. 3 mos.

Fisher, John Drinker. b. ca. 7 Oct. 1789; d. 27 Dec. 1793; age 4 yrs. 2 os. 20 dys. s/o Hendrich & Deborah Fisher.

Fitspatrick, John. b. ca. 4 Aug. 1801; d. 11 June 1803; age. 1 yr. 11 mos. 7 dys.

Fitspatrick, Peter. Native of Ballyhaise, Co. Cavan, Ireland; b. 1802; d. 2 Aug. 1832; age 30 yrs.; f/o Thomas Fitspatrick.

Fitspatrick, Thomas. 11 mos.; s/o Peter Fitspatrick.

Fitts, Aaron C. b. 1796; d. 28 Mar. 1837; age 41 yrs.

Fitts, Mrs. Mary G. b. 1789; d. 21 May 1834; age 45 yrs.; w/o A. C. Fitts.

Fitts, Virginia M. b. Aug. 1837; d. 13 Nov. 1837; age 3 mos.; d/o Aaron & Lydia Fitts.

Flake, Sarah W. b. 1812; d. 30 Jan. 1830; age 18 yrs.; d/o William & Mary Flake of Screven Co. GA.

Fletcher, Martha Ann. b. ca. Jan. 1777; d. 31 Aug. 1831; age 54 yrs. 8 mos.

Flournoy, Mary Willis. Born in GA. b. 1778; d. 8 Feb. 1830; age 52 yrs.

Flournoy, Robert Willis. b. 1803; d. 12 Feb. 1844; age 41 yrs.; Rep. to GA Leg. for Chatham Co.; had a bro.

Floyd, Elizabeth. b. ca. 1767; d. 18 Aug. 1840; age 73 yrs.

Flyming, Fingal Thomas. b. 1778; d. 29 Jan. 1814; age 36 yrs.; s/o Mary Flyming.

Flyming, Mary. b. 1727; d. 4 Oct. 1817; age 90 yrs.; m/o Fingal T. Flyming; had daus. & gr.daus.

Fogartie, Lewis Francis. Born in Charleston, SC; b. 24 Oct. 1805; d. 1 Dec. 1849; age 44 yrs. 1 mo. 7 dys.

Foley, Bryan. b. 1794; d. 3 Oct. 1849; age 55 yrs.; bro./o Daniel Foley.

Foley, Daniel. b. 1791; d. June 1835; age 44 yrs.; bro/o Bryan Foley; unc/o Francis & James Foley.

Foley, Francis. b. 1801; d. 16 Sept. 1846; age 45 yrs.; bro./o John Foley; neph/o Daniel Foley.

Foley, James. Native of Glenear, Co. Kerry, Ireland. b. 1796; d. 1 Dec. 1838; age 42 yrs.; neph/o Daniel Foley.

Foley, John. b. 1827; d. 6 Aug. 1848; age 21 yrs.; bro./o Francis Foley.

Ford, John. Native of New Jersey; b. 1780; d. 23 July 1803; age 23 yrs.; left aged father.

Fordham, John C. Native of Charleston, SC; b. ca. Aug. 1789; d. 7 Oct. 1830; age 41 yrs. 2 mos.

Forsyth, Robert Moriah. b. 1780; d. 26 July 1797; age 17 yrs.; s/o Robert & Fannie Forsyth.

Foster, Oliver. b. ca. 1765; d. 1 Oct. 1805; age 40 yrs.; unc./of George & Oliver Palmes.

Fox, Joseph. Native of Jaffrey, NH.; b.1799; d. 16 Sept. 1820; age 21 yrs.; teacher in Chatham Academy.

Frink, David, Jr. b. 1790; d. 5 Nov. 1815; age 25 yrs.; s/o David & Dezere Frink of New London, CT. Drowned.

Frink, Rev. Samuel, A.M. b. 1737; d. 4 Oct. 1773; age 36; Rector of Christ Church.

Fulton, Frances C. b. ca. 27 Feb. 1825; d. 21 Mar. 1835; age 10 yrs. 24 dys.; d/o Thomas Fulton.

Fulton, Harriet Ann E. b. ca. Mar. 1829; d.28 Sept. 1831; age 2 yrs. 6 mos.; d/o Thomas Fulton.

Fulton, Thomas. Native of Ireland; b. 1781; d. 7 July 1833; age 52 yrs.

Furth, Dr. Lewis Hermann. d. 3 June 1832. Drowned.

Ganahl, Charlotte E. b. ca. Dec. 1834; d. 23 June 1847; age 2 yrs. 7 mos.; d/o Joseph & Charlotte E. Ganahl.

Ganahl, Frederick. b. ca. Dec. 1833; d. 15 Apr. 1836; age 2 yrs. 5 mos.; s/o Joseph & Charlotte E. Ganahl.

Ganahl, George. b. ca. Dec.1830; d. 4 June 1831; age 1 yr. 6 mos.; s/o Joseph & Charlotte E. Ganahl.

Gardner, John, Jr. b. 1793; d. 28 Sept. 1827; age 34 yrs.

Gaston, William. Born in New Jersey; b. ca.1787; d. 12 Sept. 1837. Died in NY.

George, Genet. b. 29 July 1816; d. 29 Aug. 1817; d/o John B. & Ellen George.

George, Louesa. b. 29 Dec. 1817; d. 3 Sept. 1819; d/o John B. & Ellen George.

Gibbin, Thomas. b. 1766; d. 1 Oct. 1819; age 53 yrs.; left a widow.

Gibson, John. Native of SC. b. 1787; d. 28 Aug. 1820; age 33 yrs.; Yellow Fever.

Gibson, John C. Born Marion Dist. SC.

Gilbert, John H. Born in Savannah; b. 1803; d. 2 Aug. 1836.

Gilbert, William Henry. Of Hudson, NY; b. 4 May 1789; d. 13 Mar. 1816; eldest s/o Ezekiel Gilbert, Esq. & Angelica, his wife.

Gildon, Sophia. Native of New Canaan, CT; b. ca. Jan 1783; d. 5 Sept. 1827; age 44 yrs. 9 mos.; w/o Charles Gildon, Esq.

Gillespie, Bridget. b. 1808; d. 10 Aug. 1820; age 12 yrs. s/o Matilda; Yellow Fever.

Gillespie, Lt.Col. Francis. Of Marborough Dist., SC; b. 1789; d. 7 Jan. 1818; age 29 yrs. Pulmonary disease.

——————, Matilda. Native of Killesnill, Co. Leitrim, Ireland. b. ca. 1801; d. 15 Oct. 1820; age 19; w/o——————; s/o Bridget Gillespie; Yellow Fever.

Ginovoly, Mary. b. 1751; d. 6 Dec. 1812; age 61 yrs.

Gizorme, William. b. ca. 28 Aug. 1813; d. 31 Dec. 1816; age 3 yrs. 4 mos. 3 dys.

Gledhill, Mrs. Frances Ingold. Native of London, England; b. ca. 1790; d. 23 Sept. 1820; m/o James Wellington Gledhill. Yellow fever.

Gledhill, James Wellington. Born at sea, 22 June 1815; d. 2 Oct. 1820. s/o Frances I. Gledhill. Yellow Fever.

Gordon, Elizabeth Meade. b. 30 July 1764; d. 31 Jan. 1838; age 73 yrs.; wid./o Ambrose Gordon; m/o 7 chdn.; gr.gdm/Juliette Gordon Low.

Gow, Daniel Andrew. b. 1823; d. 19 Dec. 1835; s/o Andrew & Mary M. Gow.

Gow, Ellen. b. 1831; d. 21 Sept. 1834; age 3 yrs.; d/o Andrew & Mary M. Gow.

Gow, Julia. b. 1837; d. 22 Jan. 1844; age 7 yrs.; d/o Andrew & Mary M. Gow.

Gow, Susan. b. 5 Oct. 1832; d. 14 Oct. 1832; age 9 dys.; d/o Andrew & Mary M. Gow.

Gow, Susan C. b. 13 Sept. 1833; d. 20 Sept. 1834; age 1 yr. 7 dys.; d/o Andrew & Mary M. Gow.

Gray, Miss Susannah. Born New York City. b. ca. 2 June 1792; d. 26 July 1812; age 21 yrs. 1 mo. 24 dys.

Green, Mary Jane. b. 1819; d. 21 Apr. 1840.

Greene, George Washington. s/o Gen. Nathanael Greene. Drowned; Bur. Johnson Sq., Savannah, GA; d. 1793.

Greene, Gen. Nathanael. Born in RI; b. 7 Aug. 1742; died at Mulberry Grove, GA 19 June 1786; f/o George Washington Greene. Bur. Johnson Sq., Savannah, GA.

Gribben, John. Native of Antrim, Ireland; b. 1778; d. 25 Aug. 1825; age 47 yrs. Merchant in Savannah,

Gribbin, Jane. b. ca. 1726; d. 9 Mar. 1817; age 91.

Gribbin, Thomas. b. ca. 1766; d. 15 Oct. 1819.

Grimes, John, M.D. b. 1781; d. 24 June 1816; age 35 yrs.

Guerard, Anne. b. ca. 1752; died 11 July 1793; age 41; m/o 15 chdn.

Gugel, Daniel. b. 1 Nov. 1766; d. 10 Apr. 1832; h/o Mary Ann.

Gugel, Mary Ann. b. 10 Oct. 1772; d. 22 July 1847; w/o Daniel Gugel.

Gwinnett, Button. Born in Gloucestershire, England; b. ca. 1735; d. 19 May 1777; h/o Ann; f/o Elizabeth Ann; Georgia Signer of the Declaration of Independence; died as result of duel w/ Gen. Lachlan McIntosh.

Habersham, James. Born at Beverly, Yorkshire, England. Jan. 1712; d. 28 Aug. 1775, Brunswick, NJ; age 63 yrs. h/o Mary Bolton.

Habersham, Mary Bolton. d. 4 Jan. 1763; w/o James Habersham.

Haley, Mrs. Mary. Native of South Carolina; b. ca. Mar. 1791; d. 13 Apr. 1825; age 34 yrs. 1 mo.

Halligan, Catherine. b. 2 Oct. 1847; d. 10 Oct. 1847; age 8 dys.

Halligan, James. Native of Clare Morris, Co. Mayo, Ireland; b. 1814; d. 1 Mar. 1850; age 36 yrs.

Halligan, James, Jr. b. Mar. 1850; d. 4 Sept. 1850; age 6 mos.

Halligan, James. b. ca. 1853; d. 20 May 1855; age 2 yrs.; s/o Mary & Patrick Halligan.

Halligan, Mary. Native of Swinford, Co. Mayo, Ireland; b. ca. 1830; d. 6 Nov. 1855; age 25 yrs. w/o Patrick Halligan; m/o James Halligan.

Hamilton, Alexander. Native of Charleston, SC. b. 1 June 1789; d. 13 Aug. 1814; age 25 yrs. 2 mos. 12 dys.

Harden, Ann. b. ca. 1789; d. 23 Feb. 1831; age 54 yrs.; w/o Thomas Harden.

Hardwick, Charles W. Native of Jefferson Co. Ga.; b. ca. 1795; d. 6 July 1817; age 22 yrs.

Harmon, Mary V. b. ca. 27 Jan.1819; d. 29 Sept. 1819; age 10 mos.

Harmon, William H. b. ca. 9 Mar. 1822; d. 13 Feb. 1827; age 4 yrs. 10 mos. 4 dys.

Harris, Charles. Native of Charleston, SC. b. 1792; d. 26 Sept. 1809; age 17 yrs.; s/o John Hartley Harris & Mary Harris.

Harris, John Hartley. Native of Manchester, England; b. ca. 1756; d. 8 Sept. 1806; age 50 yrs.

Harris, John MacKay. Native of Charleston, SC. b. 1789; d. 25 Sept. 1804; age 15 yrs.; s/o John Hartley Harris & Mary Harris.

Harris, Mary. Native of London, England. b. 1761; d. 16 Sept. 1812; age 51 yrs.; wid./o John Hartley Harris.

Harrison, Appollos G. Native of Princeton, NJ. b. 1794; d. 23 Apr. 1815; age 21 yrs. Teacher at Savannah Academy.

Harrison, Jabez. Born in Newark, Essex Co., NJ; b. 1785; d. 18 Sept. 1808; age 23 yrs.

Harroway, Peter P. b. ca. 1792; d. 24 Oct. 1819; age 27 yrs.

Hasner, Alfred C. Born in Savannah. b. ca. 1835; d. 4 Mar. 1837.

Hasser, Andrew. Native of Germany; b. 1808; d. 23 Aug. 1840; age 32 yrs.; left a widow.

Hathaway,————. b. ca. 6 Oct. 1833; d. 16 Oct. 1834; age 1 yr. 10 dys.; inf.d/o H. B. & H. C. Hathaway.

Hayt, Lewis H. Native of Boston, MA; b. 1793; d. 18 Sept. 1823; age 30 yrs.

Heimbischer, John. Born in Savannah; b. ca. Mar. 1757; d. 31 Dec. 1804.

Henie, Mrs. Jane. Native of Ayrshire, Scotland; b. 1777; d. 5 Oct. 1815; age 38 yrs.; niece/o K. Shaw.

Henry, Albert Anthony. Born Providence, RI; b. 19 Oct. 1848; d. 18 May, 1851; age 2 yrs. 7 mos.; only child of Albert & Harriet L. Henry.

Herb, Ann Catherine. b. ca. Feb. 1764; d. 12 Oct. 1823; age 59 yrs. 10 mos.; wid/o John Herb.

Herb, Frederick. Native of Germany; b. 4 Mar. 1728; d. 26 Oct. 1790; age 62 yrs. 7 mos. 22 dys.; h/o Ursula.

Herb, Frederick. Born in Savannah; b. 1763; d. 28 Feb. 1837.

Herb, George A. b. ca. 13 Mar. 1794; d. 25 Oct. 1812; age 18 yrs. 7 mos. 12 dys.

Herb, John.

Herb, Ursula. Native of Germany; b. 28 Oct. 1741; d. 9 Nov. 1814; age 73 yrs. 12 dys.

Hersey, Naaman. Native of Hingham, MA; b. 1791; d. 22 Oct. 1817; age 26 yrs.; left wife & chdn.

Hewlett, Wyley Washington. b. ca. 22 Feb. 1811; d. 25 June 1833; age 22 yrs. 4 mos. 3 dys.

Higgins, James. Native of Parish of Chyl McCotton, Co. Sligo, Ireland; b. ca. 1781; d. 30 Aug. 1819; age 38 yrs.

Higgins, Mary. b. ca. Feb. 1817; d. 17 Nov. 1819; age 2 yrs. 7 mos.; d/o James & Catherine Higgins.

Hill, Eliza. Native of New York. b. ca. Oct. 1799; d. 21 July 1837; age 36 yrs. 10 mos.; w/o Jonathan Hill.

Hills, Mrs. Hulda. Native of Goshen, CT; b. 1797; d. 15 Apr. 1820; age 23 yrs.; w/o Levi Hills.

Hodges, Jane Ann. b. ca. 30 June 1836; d. 16 July 1837; age 1 yr. 17 dys. Inf.d/o Jilt & Julia Ann Hodges.

Hodgson, Henry. b. ca. 1770; d. 12 July 1787; age 17 yrs.; s/o Mr. Thomas Hodgson, citizen of London, England.

Hogan, John. Native of Parish of Kellenaule, Co. Tipperary, Ireland; b. 1806; d. 9 July 1851; age 45 yrs.; h/o Margaret Hogan.

Holcombe, Frances Ann. d/o John G. & Ann Holcombe.

Holcombe, H. b. ca. 1802; d. 21 Sept. 1804; age 13 mos.; s/o H. & F. Holcombe.

Holcombe, H.W. b. ca. 1800; d. 9 Feb. 1804; s/o H. & F. Holcombe.

Holcombe, W. H. b. ca. 1779; d. 22 July 1800; s/o H. & F. Holcombe.

Honiker, Robert A. b. ca. Feb. 1839; d. Apr. 1841; age 2 yrs. 2 mos.; s/o Robert A. & C. M. Honiker.

Hotchkiss, Daniel. Native of New Haven, CT; b. ca. Nov. 1788; d. 14 Sept. 1821; age 32 yrs. 10 mos. Resident of Savannah for the last 12 years; h/o Mary Ann; f/o Eliza Ann.

Hotchkiss, Eliza Ann. b. cal 1813; d. 7 Aug. 1823; age 10 yrs.

Hotchkiss, Mary Ann. b. ca. 1791; d. 29 Sept. 1823; age 32; w/o Daniel Hotchkiss; m/o Eliza Ann.

Howard, Dr. Gustavus. Born in Maryland. b. 5 July 1808; d. 20 Nov. 1832.

Howard, Jane. b. ca. 1786; d. 19 Mar. 1848; age 62 yrs.; d/o John Wallace.

Hudson, Mrs. Mary Esther. Of Screven Co., GA; b. ca. 1790; d. 18 Mar. 1821; age 31 yrs.

Hudson, Mary Lucia. b. 1 Jan. 1796; d. 16 Feb. 1833; age 37 yrs. 1 mo. 15 dys.; w/o Hamilton Hudson.

Hughson, John. b. ca. 17 Dec. 1796; d. 10 July 1817; age 21 yrs. 7 mos. 24 dys.; s/o William Hughson of Poughkeepsie, Dutchess Co., NY.

Hueston, Mrs. Selina. b. ca. 1779; d. 17 Oct. 1804; age 25 yrs.; w/o Samuel Hueston; d/o Rev. William Best; also 2 infants.

Huggins, Elizabeth. b. ca. 26 Aug. 1809; d. 5 Oct. 1840; age 31 yrs. 1 mo. 17 dys.; sis/o Sophia S. Megan.

Hulse, Justus. Native of Orange Co., NY. b. ca. 1774; d. 18 Mar. 1812; age 38 yrs.; h/o Hannah Hulse.

Hunt, Mrs. Dorcas King. Born in Pittsburg, PA; b. 2 May 1800; d. 19 Nov. 1838 at Fort Heilman, Gareys Ferry, East Florida; age 39 yrs.; w/o Lt. Col. Thomas F. Hunt, U.S. Army.

Hunter, Andrew. Born in Glasgow, N. Britain. b. ca. 1777; d. 16 Aug. 1807.

Hunter, Mrs. Eliza Ann. b. 3 Jul. 1806; d. 20 Aug. 1840; age 34 yrs. 38 dys.; w/o George Wallace Hunter.

Hunter, George Wallace. b. 15 Apr. 1806; d. 1836; age 30 yrs.

Ioor, Francis Augustus. b. ca. 21 Apr. 1819; d. 7 May 1821; age 2 yrs. 1 mo. 16 dys.; 3rd s/o William & Ann Ioor.

Isaac, Robert. Native of Glasgow, Scotland; b. 1780; d. 16 Oct. 1827; age 47 yrs.; resident of Savannah 26 yrs.; bur. in Scarbrough vault.

Jaffrey, Alexander. Native of Stirlingshire, Scotland; b. 1777; d. 9 Apr. 1810; age 33 yrs.

Jackson, Mrs. Mary Charlotte. b. Dec. 1768; d. Dec. 1807; wid./o Maj. Gen. James Jackson; d/o William & Sophia Young; niece/o Mr. & Mrs. Robert Dillon; had an infant dau.; all interred in same tomb.

James, Mrs. Mary. Born in Greenwich, NJ; b.1736; d. 28 Sept. 1818; age 82 yrs.; m/o Levi James, her youngest son.

Jenner, John. Born in York, England; b. 22 Sept. 178—; d. 5 Dec. 1808; bro./o William Jenner. Short residence in Savannah.

Johnson, Jane Dollar McCaw. b. 1785; d. 29 Jan. 1817; age 32 yrs.; w/o Thomas Johnson.

Johnston, Mrs. Bellamy. b. 1786; d. 16 Sept. 1816; age 30 yrs.; w/o William Johnson ?; same grave.

Johnston, David. Native of Glasgow, Scotland; b. 1795; d. 26 Oct. 1816; age 21 yrs.

Johnston, James. b. 27 July 1769; d. 2 July 1822.

Johnston, James. b. 1738; d. 4 Oct. 1808; age 70 yrs.; h/o Sarah Johnston.

Johnston, Lewis. b. 1779; d. 23 Oct. 1819; age 40 yrs.; h/o Sarah Johnston;? same grave.

Johnston, Mary E. b. ca. 19 Jan. 1826; d. 9 Oct. 1826; age 9 mos. 21 dys. d/o William T. & Elizabeth Johnston.

Johnston, Sarah. b. 1745; d. 26 Mar. 1815; age 70 yrs.; w/o James Johnston.

Johnston, Sarah. b. 1776; d. 1 Nov. 1820; age 44 yrs.; w/o Lewis Johnston? same grave.

Johnston, William N. b. 1785; d. 19 Oct. 1813; age 28 yrs.; same grave as Bellamy Johnston.

Jones, Miles. b. 1787; d. 7 Aug. 1820; age 33 yrs. Had wife; Yellow Fever.

Joyner, Jane W. b. 27 Apr. 1794; d. 18 Oct. 1839; wid./o William H. Joyner.

Joyner, William H. b. 9 May 1794; d. 21 Oct. 1822.

Joyner, William H. Born in Savannah. b. 1823; d. 1 Nov. 1832.

Kavanaugh, Thomas. Native of Arklow, Co. Wicklow, Ireland; b. ca. 1795; d. 7 Aug. 1833; age 38 yrs. Citizen of Savannah for many years. Left a widow.

Kean, Mrs. Mary. Native of Killaden, Co. Mayo, Ireland; b. ca. May 1831; d. 7 Feb. 1848; age 16 yrs. 9 mos.; w/o John Kean.

Kean, Martin. Native of Kilcoleman, Co. Mayo, Ireland; b. 1824; d. 24 Jan. 1847; age 23 yrs.; bro./o John Kean.

Keen, Mrs. Eliza. b. 1775; d. 28 Dec. 1822; age 47 yrs.; sis./o Michael Long.

Kerr, Rev. Robert. b. ca. 1772 or 1792; d. 11 June 1805; age 33/53 yrs.; Minister of the Associated Reformed Church.

Key, Elizabeth. Born on St. Helena Island, SC; b. ca. Jan. 1795; d. 2 Mar. 1813; age 18 yrs.2 mos.; w/o Robert Key. Childbirth.

Key, L. d. 2 Mar. 1813; age 19 yrs.

Killey, Margaret Ann. b. 8 June 1816; d. 17 June 1817; age 12 mos. 9 dys.; only d/o John & Martha Killey.

Killion, Mary. b. ca. 1814; d. 28 Aug. 1852; age 38 yrs.; wid/o Patrick Logan Killion.

Killion, Patrick Logan. Born in Galway, Ireland. b. ca. 1814; d. 17 July 1842 ; age 28 yrs.

Kimball, Richard. Of New London, CT; b.1794; d. 23 Jan. 1818; age 24 yrs.; s/o Chester & Lucy Kimball; consumption.

King, Mrs. Jane. Native of Chatham Co. GA; b. ca. 1796; d. 4 Oct. 1816; age 21; w/o John R. King of Savannah. Also newborn infant.

King, William. Native of Suffolk, England; b. ca. Nov. 1772; d. 18 Jan. 1819; age 36 yrs. 3 mos. 23 dys.; emig. to Amer. at early age; long a resid. of Savannah; left wid.

Kirby, Horace. Native of Middletown, CT; b. 1798; d. 15 June 1825; age 27 yrs.

Kirkling, Elizabeth. b. ca. 5 Feb. 1814; d. 29 Aug. 1820; age 6 yrs. 7 mos. 24 dys.

Knapp, Samuel. b. ca. 8 Feb. 1826; d. 9 Nov. 1835; age 8 yrs. 9 mos. 1 dy.; 2nd s/o H. S. & Elizabeth Knapp.

Krieger, John. b. ca. Aug. 1754; d. 26 Apr. 1800; age 45 yrs. 9 mos.

Lamar, John T. b. 1797; d. 9 July 1842; age 45 yrs.

Lamar, Lucius Henry. b. ca. Jan. 1833; d. 19 July 1834; age 18 mos.; s/o G.B. & J.M. Lamar.

Lamb, William. d. aft. 1799; age 55 yrs.; Savannah merchant.

Langton, Mary. Born in Long Island, NY. d. 14 Mar. 1819; stone erected by Levi James.

Langston, Thomas J. b. ca. 1803; d. 1 Jan. 1824; age 21 yrs.

Larkin, Mary. d. 11 July 1815; w/o Hugh Larkin.

LaRoche, Mrs. Frances S. b. 1808; d. 4 Nov. 1839; age 31 yrs.; w/o J. A. LaRoche.

Lathrop, Burrel Augustus. b. ca. 21 Aug. 1834; d. 8 Apr. 1836; age 1 yr. 8 mos. 19 dys.; s/o George A. & Sarah E. Lathrop.

Lathrop, Mary L. Louis Matilda. b. ca. 4 Jan. 1826; d. 23 June 1827; age 1 yr. 6 mos. 19 dys.

Lathrop, William. b. ca. 16 Dec. 1827; d. 4 Aug. 1828; age 8 mos. 20 dys.

Laurence, James Thompson. Born at Colerain, Ireland; b. 1759; d. 7 Sept. 1812; age 53 yrs.; lived in Savannah more than 23 yrs.

Lavinder, Dr. Mary. b. 18 Oct. 1778; d. 19 Nov. 1845; d/o Benjamin Lavinder of Burnside Island, Chatham Co. GA; first woman doctor in GA.

Lawlor, Honora. b. 1786; d. 4 Aug. 1820; age 34 yrs.; w/o John Lawlor; Yellow Fever.

Lawlor, John. Native of Co. Carlow, Ireland; b. 1785; d. 4 June 1820; age 35 yrs.; h/o Honora Lawlor; Yellow Fever.

Lawrance, James. b. ca. 7 Jan. 1841; d. 28 Feb. 1842; age 1 yr. 1 mo. 21 dys.; inf. s/o Peter & Abigail Lawrance of New York.

Lawton, Mrs. Elizabeth M. b. ca. 1809; d. 28 Oct. 1839; age 30 yrs.

Lawton, Hannah. b. ca. 1786; d. 4 Aug. 1820; age 34 yrs.; Yellow Fever.

Lawton, John. Born in Carlow, Ireland; b. ca. 1786; d. 4 June 1820; age 34 yrs.; Yellow Fever.

Leahy, Mr. Michael. Native of Cork, Ireland; b. 1795; d. 5 Oct. 1820; age 25 yrs. Yellow Fever.

Leake, Richard, Esq. b. ca. 1747; d. 25 Mar. 1802; age 55 yrs.

Leaver, Gabriel. b. ca. 1757; d. 23 Oct. 1795; age 38 yrs.; h/o Mary Schick; f/o Mary Leaver Marshall; cabinet maker. (Moved to Laurel Grove Cemetery, 1855.)

Lee, Thomas Y. Native of New York

LeForce, Hiram. b. ca. 1815; d. 26 Oct. 1817; age 2 yrs.

Leggett, Sarah W. b. ca. 1790; d. 30 Nov. 1791; age 1 yr.

LeGriel, Nerestan. Born Port Au Prince, St. Domingue; b. 1 Jan.. 1838; d. 16 Jan 1838; age 39 yrs.

LeGriel, Onesime. Born at St. Marc, Island of St. Domingue; b. 29 Dec. 1802; d. 5 Mar. 1840; age 38 yrs. 2 mos.; left wife & chdn.

LeMoine, Abbe Jean Baptiste. Born in France; Cure of Marly LeRoi, France; came to America 1792; d. 1794; First Roman Catholic priest in Savannah.

Lillibridge, Mrs. Abigail. b. 1759; d. 3 Dec. 1796; age 37 yrs.; w/o Mr. John Lillibridge of Newport, RI; also her inf. son.

Lillibridge, Hampton Baxter. b. ca. 10 June 1792; d. 18 Sept. 1817; age 25 yrs. 3 mos. 8 dys.

Linder, Mrs. Jane Elizabeth. b. 21 Dec. 1822; d. 3 Sept. 1839; age 16 yrs. 8 mos. 12 dys.; w/o James F. Linder.

Little, Henry Mather. Native of East Cowes, Isle of Wight, England; b. 1796; d. 31 Aug. 1833; age 37 yrs.

Livingston, Dr. Charles O. Of New York; b. 1805; d. 16 Apr. 1832; age 27 yrs.

Lloyd, Mrs. Caroline. b. ca. Apr. 1765; d. 5 Dec. 1836; age 71 yrs. 8 mos.; w/o W. H. Lloyd.

Lloyd, I. Wallace. b. ca. Jan. 1820; d. 18 Oct. 1820; s/o Thomas Edward Lloyd; Yellow Fever.

Lloyd, Thomas Edward. b. ca. 1789; d. 11 Sept. 1820; age 31 yrs.; Yellow Fever.

Logan, Mary F. Native of Parish of Killion, Co. Galway, Ireland; b. ca. 1814; d. 26 Aug. 1852; age 38 yrs. w/o Patrick Logan; m/o Sarah Ann Logan.

Logan, Michael. Native of Balanghleagh Parish of Killaughen, Co. Galway, Ireland; b. 1826; d. 2 July 1851; age 25 yrs.; h/o Sarah Logan.

Logan, Patrick. Native of Parish of Killion, Co. Galway, Ireland; b. ca. 1814; d. 17 July 1842; age 28 yrs.; h/o Mary F. Logan; f/o Sarah Ann.

Long, Michael. b. 1782; d. 13 mar. 1824; age 42 yrs. bro./o Mrs. Eliza Keen.

Long, Henry. b. 6 Mar. 1817; d. 15 Nov. 1837; age 20 yrs.

Long, Michael. b. ca. 1782; d. 13 Mar. 1824; age 42 yrs.

Long, Mrs. Mary E. b. ca. 1784; d. 12 Sept. 1846; age 62 yrs.

Lucas, Lucinda. b. ca. 1729; d. 6 Mar. 1812; age 83 yrs.

Ludington, Charlotte. b. ca. 1813; d. 13 Mar. 1840; age 27 yrs.; w/o William S. Ludington; had 1 chd.

Ludlow, Miss Phebe. Native of New Jersey; b. ca. Oct. 1807; d. 13 June 1826; age 18 yrs. 9 mos.

Ludlum, Cornelius. Native of New Jersey; b. 1775; d. 8 Jan. 1804; age 29 yrs.; drowned w/ John Tucker & Joseph White.

Luther, Thomas. Native of Swansey, MA; b. ca. 1792; d. 30 June 1830.

Lynch, Charles Humphreys. b. ca. 30 Jan. 1818; d. 20 Dec. 1818; age 10 mos. 21 dys.; s/o William & Ann Jane Lynch of Lynchburg, VA.

McAlister, Ellen. b. ca. 1750; d. 29 Oct. 1802; age 52 yrs.

McAlister, Hercules. b. ca. 1787; d. 30 Oct. 1802; age 15 yrs.

McAlister, William. b. ca. 1807; d. 6 Feb. 1832; age 25 yrs.; s/o S. & Rose McAlister of Ballycastle, Ireland.

McAllister, Clementina I. b. ca. Mar. 1807; d. 18 July 1834; age 24 yrs. 5 mos.

McAllister, Louisa Caroline. b. ca. 4 Jan. 1801; d. 23 Mar. 1803; age 2 yrs. 2 mos. 19 dys.; only chd./o Mrs. Louisa McAllister, wid./o Richard McAllister.

McCall, Hugh, Maj. Born in NC. d. 10 June 1824; Brevet Major, U.S. Army.

McCann, Mrs. Mahalah. Native of Danville, VA; b. ca. Sept. 1820; d. Nov. 1850; age 30 yrs. 2 mos.; w/o James McCann.

McCartney, Bridget. Native of Ireland, Co. of South; b. 1795; d. 9 Sept. 1820; w/o Patrick McCartney; m/o John McCartney; age 25 yrs.; Yellow Fever.

McCartney, John. age 2 yrs. 2 mos.; s/o Patrick & Bridget McCartney.

McDermott, James. Native of Co. Roscommon, Ireland; Resident of Philadelphia, PA; b. 1770; d. 26 Aug. 1809; age 30 yrs.; bro./o John McDermott of Philadelphia; died in Savannah.

McDonald, Christopher. b. 1802; d. 1 Mar. 1844; age 42 yrs.; left widow.

McFarland, William. b. ca. Jan. 1766; d. 17 Nov. 1815; age 49 yrs. 10 mos.

McGurk, Patrick. Of the Parish of Grannard, Co. Longford, Ireland; b. 1794; d. 24 Oct. 1825; age 31 yrs.; bro./o Francis & Thomas McGurk.

McHale, John. b. ca. 6 May 1841; d. 6 June 1841; age 1 mo.; s/o Patrick & Ellen McHale.

McIntyre, Andrew. Born in Ireland. b. 1800; d. 5 Apr. 1847.

McIntosh, Maj. Gen. Lachlan. b. 17 Mar. 1725; d. 20 Feb. 1806.

McKinnon, Martha A. b. ca. 31 Oct. 1818; d. 10 Mar. 1847; age 28 yrs. 6 mos. 10 dys.; w/o R.W. McKinnon.

McKinnon, Robert Bruce. b. ca. be. 1847; d. 2 Apr. 1847; age 1 mo.10 dys.; s/o R.W. & Martha A. McKinnon.

McKinnon, William Wallace. b. ca. 14 Apr. 1845; d. 17 Aug. 1847; age 2 yrs. 4 mos. 3 dys.; s/o R.W. & M.A. McKinnon.

McLaughlin, Mrs. Ann. Born in SC b. 4 Oct. 1753; d. 8 Dec. 1839; age 86 yrs. 2 mos. 4 dys.

McMillan, Samuel. Native of Charleston, SC; b. ca. Mar. 1793; d. 11 Sept. 1815. Had a brother.

McMurrin, Charles. b. 1788; d. 12 Oct. 1810; age 22 yrs.

McQueen, Mrs. Anne. d. 24 Mar. 1809; m/o Eliza McQueen Mackay.

McQueen, John (Don Juan). b. 1773; d. 1822.

MacKay, Capt. John. b. 1806; d. 31 May 1848; age 42 yrs.; U.S. Corps of Topographical Engineers.

Maitland, Lt. Col. John. Born in Laude, Scotland; b. 1732; d. 25 Oct. 1779; remains returned to Scotland in 1981; Malaria.

Malaurie, Marie Elizabeth. b. 23 Aug. 1749; d. 11 Nov. 1842.

Malbone, Edward Greene. b. 1778; d. 7 May 1807; age 29. s/o Gen. John Malbone of Newport, RI.

Mallette, George W. b. ca. 1 Oct. 1846; d. 22 Mar. 1847; age 6 mos. 22 dys.; s/o John D. & E. A. Mallette.

Mann, Michael C. Native of Parish of Killofin, Co. Clare, Ireland b. 1797; d. 17 Oct. 1819; age 22 yrs.; bro/o Catherine Mann Desmond.

Mark, Elizabeth S. b. 1796; d. 9 Sept. 1817; age 21 yrs.; gd/o Ann Prince.

Masterton, James T. b. 15 June 1822; d. 12 Nov. 1832.

Masterton, William. b. ca. 1798; d. 14 Sept. 1824. Stonecutter.

Mazyck, Thomas Winstanly. b. 1812; d. 21 Sept. 1827; age 15 yrs.; s/o Dr. Thomas Mazyck of Charleston, SC.

Mealy, Stephen Albion. b. 3 Feb. 1833; d. 11 June 1834; inf.s/o Rev. S.A. & C. A. Mealy.

Megan, Charles J. b. ca. Aug. 1800; d. 3 Oct. 1842; age 42 yrs.; h/o Sophia S. Megan.

Meldrum, Alex. Native of Scotland; b. 1808; d. 11 Jan. 1837; age 29 yrs.

Melvin, Robert. Of Quebec; b. ca. 1784; d. 3 Dec. 1830; age 46 yrs.

Mendenhall, Thomas, Esq. b. ca. June 1750; d. 2 Oct. 1808; age 58 yrs. 6 mos.; cashier of Office of Discount & Deposit in Savannah.

Meriam, Augusta Maria. b. 1795; d. 23 Sept. 1829; age 25 yrs.; d/o Dr. Asa & Mrs. Mary Meriam, of MA.

Merriman, Charles. Born in Watertown, CT. b. 1799; d. 10 July 1835; age 36 yrs.

Millen, John. b. ca. 1757; d. 28 Oct. 1811; age 54 yrs.

Millen, Rosannah. b. ca. 1752; d. 20 Feb. 1810; age 58.

Millen, Thomas. Born in Great Britain; b. 1732; d. 27 Sept. 1784 in Savannah; left w.

Miller, John Phillip. d. 24 Apr. 1794.

Miller, George W. Of Savannah; b. 1818; d. 9 Sept. 1851; age 33 yrs.; d. in New York

Miller, Mrs. Mary. b. 4 July 1786; d. 31 Jan. 1840.

Miller, Odrey. Native of Scott Co., KY; b. ca. Apr. 1798; d. 13 July 1831; killed in duel with Michael Brown. Shot in the head.

Miller, Sarah. Born in Baltimore, MD; b. ca. 1792; d. 3 Oct. 1817; age 25 yrs.; w/o Jacob Miller.

Milligan, Michael. Born in Ireland; b. ca. 1774; d. 5 Jan. 1805; age 35 yrs.

Mills, Archibald. b. 28 Dec. 1764; d. 26 Feb. 1818.

Mills, John Richmond. b. ca. 1786; d. 28 Sept. 1812 (?); age 26 yrs.

Mills, Reginald.

Mills, Thomas Lewis. b. ca. June 1817; d. 19 July 1818; age 13 mos.; s/o Jacob & Sarah Mills.

Mills, William C. b. ca. 1790; d. 6 Nov. 1827; age 37 yrs.

Mitchell, Eliza C. Born in Savannah. b. ca. Dec. 1819; d. 30 July 1836; age 16 yrs. 10 mos.; w/o Dr. J. J. Mitchell.

Mitchell, Robert. Born Perth, N. Britain.; b. 1 July 1776; d. 26 Dec. 1830; merchant in Savannah.

Moore, John. b. ca. 1770; d. 24 Sept. 1797; age 27 yrs.

Moore, Sumner. Late of NH; b. 1803; d. 30 Sept. 1825; age 22 yrs.; stonecutter.

Moorhouse, Mrs. Mary. b. ca. 1776; d. 29 Aug. 1809; age 33; w/o Mr. Ralph A. Moorhouse of Chelmsford, England.

Moorhouse, Ralph Story. b.1808; d. 11 Sept. 1808; age 9 wks.; s/o Ralph & Mary Moorhouse.

Mordecai, David M. d. 29 Sept. 1819; s/o Samuel & Caroline Mordecai.

Mordecai, Matilda E. b. ca. Apr. 1807; d. 11 Sept. 1819; age 12 yrs. 5 mos.; d/o Samuel & Caroline Mordecai.

Morecock, Catharine. b. ca. Sept. 1743; d. 13 Feb. 1813; age 69 yrs. 5 mos.

Mordecai, Astel H. b. ca. Aug. 1790; d. Feb. 1813; age 22 yrs. 6 mos. 11 dys.

Morel, Charles Harris. b. ca. 30 Nov. 1798; d. 18 Oct. 1820; age 21 yrs. 11 mos. 18 dys.

Morel, Hannah. b. ca. 22 May 1776; d. 5 Apr. 1790; age 13 yrs. 11 mos. 15 dys.; d/o the late John Morel, Esq.; fell from horse.

Morel, John H. Born in Savannah; b. ca. 1781; d. 3 June 1834.

Morel, Margaret. b. 8 Aug. 1812; d. 18 Nov. 1821; d/o Peter Henry & Ann Morel; sis/o James S. Morel.

Morel, Richard. Native of Newtown, Long Island, NY. b. 1780; d. 2 Feb. 1816; age 36 yrs.

Morin, Mary Anne Victoire Armaignac. Native of St. Domingue; b. 1774; d. 12 Mar 1806; age 33 yrs.; w/o Pierre Morin; sis/o Claire Adelaide Armaigmac D'Espinose.

Morningstar, Henry. b. 1793; d. 1 Oct. 1833; age 40 yrs.

Morris, Samuel. Native of Newark, NJ; b. ca. 1780; d. 19 July 1810; age 30 yrs.; s/o John & Sarah Morris.

Moxham, Thomas F. Native of Savannah, GA. b. 1795; d. 14 June 1838; age 43 yrs.; stone erected by Mrs. Sophia S. Megan.

Muir, Josiah. b. 1779; d. 1 Oct. 1820; age 41 yrs. h/o Mary; Yellow Fever.

Muir, Lewis Phoenix. b. 1812; d. 18 Oct. 1820; age 12 yrs.; s/o Josiah & Mary Muir. Yellow Fever.

Muir, Mary. b. 1776; d. 25 Aug. 1823; age 47 yrs. w/o Josiah Muir.

Mulvey, Jacob. d. 1823; age 29 yrs.; s/o Charles Mulvey of Philadelphia, PA.

Muzzall, Isaac S. K. Native of London, C.B.; b. ca. Mar. 1779; d. 2 Oct. 1805; age 26 yrs. 5 mos.; left widow.

Neckerson, Bethiah. b. ca. 1761; d. 13 oct. 1799; age 38 yrs.; wid./o Ely Neckerson.

Nelligan, Michael. Native of Ireland b. 1774; d. 5 Jan. 1809; age 35 yrs.

Nelson, Thomas. b. ca . 1774; d. 21 Dec. 1808; age 34 yrs.

Neville, Mr. Peter. Native of Halifax, Nova Scotia; b. 1790; d. 30 Nov. 1820; Yellow Fever.

Newell, Alanson. Native of Greenfield, MA. b. ca. Mar. 1811; d. 12 Aug. 1835; age 24 yrs. 5 mos.

Newcomb, Mrs. Abigail. Native of Boston, MA. b. ca. Apr. 1780; d. 7 Oct. 1817; age 37 yrs. 6 mos.; w/o Capt. Reuben Newcomb; m/o Maria Emmaline Ocain.

Newcomb, Maria Emmaline Ocain. b. ca, Jan. 1806; d. ca. 10 Oct. 1817; age 11 yrs. 9 mos.; d/o Capt. Reuben & Mrs. Abigail Newcomb; died 38 hrs. after mother.

Newman, Mrs. Catherine. Born in Westford, Mass.; b. Nov. 1793; d. 12 Oct. 1824; age 31 yrs.; w/o William Newman.

Newton, John. Native of Mancester, England; b. ca. Aug. 1801; d. 11 June 1820; age 18 (?) yrs. 10 mos.

Neyle, William. Native of England; b. ca. 1768; d. Dec. 1802; age 34 yrs. Left wife & two infant daus.

Norris, Sarah Hill. b. 1805; d. 6 June 1835; age 30 yrs. w/o James B. Norris; m/o 2 inf. chdn., also bur. with her.

Norris, John R. Born in Tarrytown, NY; b. 1778; d. Nov. 1803.

Norris, Thomas Benjamin. age 1 dy.; inf.s/o James B. & Sarah Hill Norris.

Norton, Capt.William. Of South Carolina; b. ca. 1773; d. 23 Mar. 1834; age 60 yrs. 10 mos.

O'Byrne, Mary B. b. 1812; d. 3 Jan.1836; age 24 yrs.; w/o Mr. Lawrence O'Byrne; d/o Mr. Myles Dempsey of Charleston, SC.; m. Lawrence O'Byrne in 1832; Catholic; m/o James Jeremiah O'Byrne.

O'Byrne, infant daughter. d/o Lawrence & Mary B. O'Byrne.

O'Byrne, Patrick. d. 1801.

O'Connor, Arthur Patrick. Native of Ennis, Co. Clare, Ireland; b. ca. 1792; d. 10 Apr. 1820; age 28 yrs.; left a wife.

O'Connor, —————. w/o Michael O'Connor.

Odingsells, Maj. Charles. b. 1754; d. 2 Dec. 1810; age 56 yrs.; Rev. soldier; legislator; farmer; d. on Skidaway Island.

Odingsells, Charles Spencer. b. ca. 11 Mar. 1811; d. 17 Oct. 1817; age 6 yrs. 7 mos. 6 dys.; s/o Charles Odingsells, Esq.

Odingsells, Mary Susannah. b. ca. 31 Oct. 1808; d. 6 Nov. 1817; age 9 yrs. 7 dys.; d/o Charles Odingsells, Esq.

Oglebay, Georgia. b. 1824; d. 14 Oct. 1851; age 27 yrs.; Adopted d/o William & Ann C. Oglebay.

Oglebay, William. b. 1780; d. 17 June 1829; age 49 yrs.

O'Keefe, Mary Ann. b. ca. 1804; d. 7 Jan. 1808; age 4 yrs.; eld. d/o Patrick & Mary O'Keefe.

O'Keefe, Mary Colbert. b. 1764; d. 11 Oct. 1809; age 45 yrs. w/o Patrick O'Keefe.

O'Keefe, William John. youngest s/o Patrick & Mary C. O'Keefe.

Oliver, George. 1841.

Oliver, Capt. John. Native of Isle of Leon; b. 1814; d. 22 July 1836; age 57 yrs.

Olmstead, Nathaniel H. Born in CT; b. ca. 1791; d. 5 Jan. 1832; age 41; was married, had children, also had a brother.

Orme, John. b. 1768; d. 1820; yellow fever.

Orme, John, M.D. b. 1821; d. 8 Apr. 1848; age 27 yrs.

Orme, John, Jr. b. 1804; d. 1826; s/o John Orme.

Orme, Mary M. b. 1800; d. 1820; d/o John Orme; yellow fever.

Owens, George. Born in Savannah; b. 1817; d. 17 Jan. 1821.

Palmer, Lewis M. Born in GA; d. 12 Nov. 1846.

Palmer, Thomas B. Born Co. Tipperary, Prov. of Munster, Ireand; b. ca. 16 Aug. 1786; d. 30 Dec. 1811; age 25 yrs. 4 mos. 14 dys. Lived in U.S. 13 yrs.; died in Savannah of consumption.

Palmes, Daniel Baker. b. Aug. 1828; d. 16 Sept. 1828; age 1 mo.; s/o George F. & Caroline L. Palmes.

Parisot, Augustus Claudius. b. ca. 19 Jan. 1833; d. 1 June 1835; age 17 mos. 14 dys.; s/o John F. & Maria L. Parisot.

Parker, George. age 2 yrs.; s/o Ann Parker.

Parr, Stephen. Native of Orange Co. NY. b. ca. 29 Nov. 1824; d. 17 Jan. 1838; age 13 yrs. 1 mo. & 20 dys.

Parsons, Ignatius. Native of Cape Ann, MA; b. ca. 1789; d. 29 Dec. 1825; age 36 yrs.

Patrick, Thomas. d. 8 Feb. 1849.

Patterson, Ann. b. ca. 1 Jan. 1791; d. 8 Apr. 1816; age 25 yrs. 3 mos. 8 dys.; w/o William Patterson.

Patterson, Ann T. b. 1791; d. 8 July 1813; age 22 yrs.; w/o Thomas M. Patterson.

Patterson, C. (or G.) H. b. 1791; d. 27 Oct. 1820; age 29 yrs. Yellow fever.

Patterson, Eleanor. b. ca. Apr. 1805; d. 28 Nov. 1813; age 8 yrs. 7 mos.; d/o James & Susan Patterson.

Patterson, Janett. b. 1742; d. 5 Dec. 1815; age 73 yrs.

Patterson, Capt. William. Native of Philadelphia, PA.; b. 11 Feb. 1788; d. 14 Aug. 1812.

Pearce, Milledge. b. 1800; d. 16 Oct. 1817.

Peigne, Aug-jne-esth. Born in Larcahaye, St. Domingue; b. 8 July 1784; d. 2 Sept 1816.

Pelot, Charles Edward. b. 12 Feb. 1839; d. 26 Mar. 1839; 2 nd s/o William M. & Rosalie Pelot.

Pelot, Joseph S. b. ca. 1 Feb. 1791; d. 16 Oct. 1833; age 42 yrs. 9 mos. 16 dys.

Perkins, Edward. Native of Hartford, CT; b. 1785; d. 18 Nov. 1826; age 41 yrs.; left widow & 5 daus.; merchant in Savannah.

Perkins, Miss Sylvania Truman. b. 1795; d. 3 July 1808; age 13 yrs.; d/o Daniel & Ann Perkins of Ashford, CT.

Pettigrew, Elizabeth O. Heriot. b. ca. 1794; d. 17 Oct.1820; age 26 yrs.; w/o Alexander Pettigrew, M.A. He was a teacher in Savannah and late writer in Glasgow, Scotland.

Petty, Eliza Francis. b. 29 Jan. 1824; d. 9 July 1827; age 2 mos. 11 dys. d/o Lazarus & Sarah Petty.

Petty, James B. b. ca. 17 Oct. 1827; d. 28 Dec. 1827; age 2 mos. 11 dys. s/o Lazarus & Sarah Petty.

Petty, William Wright. b. 11 Jan. 1826; d. 23 Aug. 1830; s/o Lazarus & Sarah Petty.

Phelan, Patrick. Native of Ballyporeen, Co. Tipperary, Ireland; d. 10 Oct. 1812; left wife.

Pidge, Louisa M. b. ca. Nov. 1820; d. 28 July 1826; age 5 yrs. 10 mos.; d/o David & Eliza Pidge.

Pierce, Julia Foster. b. ca. 23 Oct. 1836; d. 7 Dec. 1837; age 14 mos. 15 dys.; youngest d/o Rev. George F. & Ann M. Pierce.

Pierce, William Leigh. b. ca. 1740; d. 10 Dec. 1789. Framer of the Constitution of the United States.

Pindar, Mrs. Melinda. b. 1780; d. 24 July 1852; age 72 yrs.; aunt/o Miss Phillips of Manchester, England.

Pinder, Rebecca Harriot. b. ca. Sept 1790; d. 25 July 1791; age 11 mos.; d/o William & Rebecca Pinder/Pindar.

Pinto, Richard Julia S. b.1787; d. 2 Apr. 1818; age 31 yrs.; oldest s/o Gaston Puito Silva of the Island of Madeira.

Pitman, Richard H. b. 1806; d. 7 Oct. 1839; age 33 yrs.

Pittman, James A. b. 25 Feb. 1829; d. 27 June 1831.

Pitman, Virginia Ann. b. 11 Jan. 1831; d. 5 Nov. 1831; age 9 mos. 24 dys.; d/o R.H. & A.C. Pitman.

Pitts, Hardy G. b. ca. Jan. 1786; d. 29 Apr. 1840; age 54 yrs. 3 mos.

Ponyat, Marie Lamaignere. Native of St. Domingue b. 1774; d. 12 Mar. 1806; age 32 yrs.; w/o Jean Francois Ponyat; niece/o Jerome Francois & Claire Adelaide Armaignac D'Espinose.

Poince, James. b. ca. 23 May 1814; d. 9 June 1849; age 35 yrs. 18 dys.; left wife; accidental shooting.

Powers, Titus. Of Middletown, CT; b. ca. 1774; d. 26 July 1796; age 22 yrs.; b/o William and Danter Powers.

Powers, William. Of Middletown, CT; b. ca. 1776; d. 1 Oct. 1804; age 28 yrs.; b/o Titus and Danter Power.

Poythress, Hetty A. d. 24 Dec. 1818; w/o George Poythress of Burke Co., GA.

Prendergast, David. Native of Parish of Gilcoma, Co. Mayo, Ireland; b. 1796; d. 21 July 1820; age 24 yrs.; bro./o John & Michael Prendergast; yellow fever.

Prince, Ann. Born in SC; b. 1748; d. 29 Oct. 1817; age 69 yrs.; gm/o Elizabeth S. Mark.

Price, Thomas R. Native of Newark, NJ; b. 1792; d. 22 Feb. 1827; age 35 yrs.

Pridgeon, M.L.D. b. ca. Apr. 1821; d. 27 Sept. 1850; age 29 yrs. 5 mos.

Purse, Anna A. b. 5 May 1836; d. 18 Apr. 1838; d/o Thomas & Eliza Jane Purse.

Purse, Catherine Ann. b. 5 Feb. 1838; d. 5 Feb. 1838; d/o Thomas & Eliza Jane Purse.

Purse, Esther M. b. 25 Sept. 1845; d.19 Oct. 1845; d/o Thomas & Eliza Jane Purse.

Purse, Frances. b. Feb. 1849; d. 24 Sept. 1849; d/o Thomas & Eliza Jane Purse.

Purse, Margaret M. b. 25 Sept. 1846; d. 7 Aug. 1847; d/o Thomas & Eliza Jane Purse.

Purse, Mary Pilkington. Born in Baltimore, MD; b. 1 May 1777; d. 3 July 1848; died in Savannah.; wid. of Thomas Purse, Sr.

Purse, Mary E. b. 28 June 1829; d. 28 Nov. 1829; d/o Thomas & Eliza Jane Purse.

Ralston, —————. b. ca. 1771; d. 13 Sept. 1814; age 43 yrs.

Ralston, Catherine. b. ca. May 1811; d. 28 Sept. 1814; age 3 yrs. 4 mos.; eldest d/o John & Rosetta Ralston.

Rapp, Catharine. b.1794; d. 29 July 1823; age 29 yrs.; w/o Charles F. Rapp.

Rapp, Charles F. b. 20 Oct. 1822; d. 28 Oct. 1822; age 8 dys. s/o Charles F. & Catharine Rapp.

Rapp, Louisa. b. ca. June 1821; d. 2 Oct. 1823; 2 yrs. 4 mos.; d/o Charles F. & Catharine Rapp.

Ratcliff, Richard. Native of Glynn Co., GA; b. 1777; d. 16 Aug. 1804; age 27 yrs.

Ravot, Vivien. Born in France; b. ca. 1777; d. 4 Sept. 1804; age 27 yrs.; Lt. of Fr. Corvette *L'Amitie.*

Rawls, Rev. Thomas J. Born in Screven Co., GA. b. June 1817; d. 15 Sept. 1839; age 22 yrs. 3 mos.; neph./o Mrs. E.G. Abbott; Missionary to people of color on Back River. Died in Savannah.

Ray, William. b. ca. 13 June 1799; d. 24 Apr. 1811; age 12 yrs. 11 mos.; s/o Capt. Nathaniel Ray of Philadelphia; fell from mast of brig *America.*

Raymond, George A. b. 1794; d. 26 Nov. 1821; age 27 yrs.

Reilly, Christopher. Native of Athboy, Co. Meath, Ireland; b. 1789; d. June 1820; age 31; bro./o Richard Reilly, et.al.; yellow fever.

Reilly, Richard. Native of Athboy, Co. Meath, Ireland; b. 1791; d. June 1820; age 29; bro./o Christopher Reilly, et.al.; yellow fever.

Remington, Charles. b. ca. May 1799; d. 2 Nov. 1819; age 20 yrs. 6 mos.; s/o the late Capt. Charles & Mrs. Mary Remington of Pawtuxet, RI.

Remington, Charlie, Jr. d. 1819.

Riberon, Josefin. b. ca. 24 Dec. 1826; d. 30 Sept. 1830; age 3 yrs. 9 mos. 6 dys.

Richardson,William, Sr. b. 1772; d. 14 Oct. 1827; age 55 yrs. Had w. & chdn.

Ricker, Shapleigh. Native of Portsmouth, NH. b. 1790; d. 15 Aug. 1819; age 29 yrs. 9 dys.; left. wid. & 1 chd.

Riggs, Nathaniel Evans. Born in Savannah; b. 3 May 1813; d. 30 Oct. 1813; s/o William & R.E. Riggs.

Robert, Henry E. b. ca. Nov. 1841; d. 7 Aug. 1842; age 10 mos.

Robert, M. S. b. ca. 16 Jan. 1772; d. 2 Nov. 1802; age 30 yrs. 10 mos. 18 dys.; w/o G. Robert; mother of G. Robert's 6 chdn.

Robert, William P. Born in Savannah; b. ca. 4 Nov. 1837; d. 11 Nov. 1839; age 2 yrs. 7 dys.

Roberts, M. E. b. ca. Mar. 1808; d. 2 Sept. 1823; age 15 yrs. 6 mos.; d/o James & Mary Roberts.

Roberts, Mrs. Sally. Native of New Jersey; b. ca. 1788; d. 30 Aug. 1806; age 18 yrs. 21. dys.; w/o Mr. Moses A. Roberts.

Roberts, Lt. M. A. Native of Newark, NJ. b. 1784; d. 1815; 8th Reg. Inf. U.S.A.

Roberts, Samuel G. Of Boston, MA; b. 1779; d. Oct. 1805; age 26 yrs.

Robertson, F. E. d. 5 Apr. 1846.

Robins, Isaac H. b. 1787; d.3 Sept. 1820; age 33 yrs.; f/o Sarah C. H. Robins. Yellow fever.

Robins, Sarah C. H. b. 1799; d. 3 Sept. 1820; age 1 yr.; d/o Isaac H. Robins. Yellow fever.

Robinson, John. b. 1774; d. 20 Sept. 1840; age 66 yrs.; h/o Martha Robinson; d. at Newark, NJ.

Robinson, Mrs. Martha. b. 1781; d. 21 Aug. 1845; age 64 yrs.; wid. of John Robinson.

Robinson, Stephen Cook. b. 1808; d. 24 Dec. 1825; s/o John & Martha Robinson.

Roma, Mrs. Marie A.V. Fritot. b. 1755; d. 24 Dec. 1817; age 62 yrs.; w/o Francis Roma of Savannah; left a hus. & a surviving dau.

Ross, Silas. Of Whitfield, NJ; b. ca. 24 Oct. 1794; d. 19 Sept. 1820; age 26 yrs. 11 mos. 27 dys.; left wife & chd.; s/o Abner Ross.

Rowson, Charlotte. b. 1769; d. 20 Sept. 1815; age 46; w/o John E. Rowson; d/o Rev. John Beverly of Kingstown-Upon-Hull, England.

Royston, Mrs. Bridget. Native of Carricksonsuir, Ireland. b. 1782; d. 28 Oct. 1806; age 24 yrs.; w/o Capt. William Royston.

Russell, Carolina Eliza. b. 11 Jan. 1842; d. 7 Oct. 1843; d/o A. & A. E. Russell.

Russell, Joseph A. b. 1784; d. 7 Jan. 1833; age 51 yrs.

Russell, Mary Ann Elizabeth. b. 9 June 1840; d. 13 Oct. 1843; d/o A. & A. E. Russell.

Sake, Daniel W. Native of Staten Island, NY; b. 1789; d. 18 July 1820; age 31 yrs.

Santini, Harriet E. Born in Savannah; b. 1846; d. ca. 8 Sept 1848.

Santini, Female infant. Born in Savannah; b. ca. Aug. 1848; d. ca. 28 Sept. 1848.

Sawyer, William. b. ca. 1765; d. 27 July 1811; age 46 yrs.

Scarbrough, Julia Bernard. Born in Wilmington, NC; d. 16 Dec. 1856; m. William Scarbrough 1801; wid./o William Scarbrough, Esq.

Scarbrough, William, Esq. Born near Beaufort, SC. b. 18 Feb. 1776; d. 11 June 1838 in New York City; age 63 yrs.; bur. in Savannah, GA, 15 June 1839.

Schaefer, John Dieterich. Late of Philadelphia. b. 10 July 1753; d. 26 Sept. 1773; age 20 yrs. 2 mos. 2 wks.; s/o David & Catherine Schaefer.

Schenk, Peter. Born in New Jersey; b. 16 Jan. 1787; d. 20 June 1823; age 36 yrs.; resident of Savannah 17 yrs.

Scott, Gavin. Native of North Briton; b. ca. May 1767; d. 5 Jan. 1812; age 45 yrs. 8 mos.; hairdresser.

Screven, John. b. ca. 1777; d. Nov. 1830; age 53 yrs.; h/o Sarah Ann.

Screven, Sarah Ann. b. ca. 1788; d. June 1823; age 35 yrs.; second w/o John Screven.

Scribner, Abraham Webster. b. ca. 1765; d. 19 Sept. 1817; age 52 yrs.; h/o Margaret; f/o Sarah Harmon Scribner & James Benjamin Scribner.

Scribner, James Benjamin. b. ca. 1810 (?); d. 20 Jan. 1816; only s/o Abraham & Margaret Scribner.

Scribner, Margaret S. b. ca. 1792; d. 10 Apr. 1817; age 25 yrs.; w/o Abraham W. Scribner; m/o Sarah Harmon Scribner & James Benjamin Scribner.

Scribner, Sarah Harmon. b. ca. 1810; d. 16 July 1814; age 4 yrs. 6 mos.; only dau. of Abraham & Margaret Scribner.

Secord, David. Of St. David's, Upper Canada; b. ca. 3 Aug. 1794; d. 7 Apr. 1821; age 26 yrs. 8 mos. 4 dys.; h/o Margaret; f/o David Hiram Secord.

Secord, David Hiram. Infant. b. July 1820; d. 8 Nov. 1820; age 3 mos. 27 dys.; s/o David & Margaret Secord; yellow fever.

Secord, Margaret. b. Jan. 1801; d. 16 Sept. 1820; age 19 yrs. 8 mos.; w/o David Secord; d/o Timothy & Catharine Herbert of New York; m/o David Hiram Secord; yellow fever.

Seset, Matilda M. b. ca. 9 Apr. 1830; d. 24 July 1837; age 5 yrs. 3 mos. 16 dys.

Seymour, Gordon Isaac. Native of Hartford, CT; b. 8 July 1773; d. 13 Sept. 1814; age 41 yrs. 2 mo. 5 dys.; h/o Catherine Seymour; f/o Gordon Seymour. Resided in Savannah 20 yrs.

Seymour, Gordon. b. ca. 17 Apr. 1807; d. 28 May 1808; age 13 mos. 11 dys.; s/o Gordon & Catherine Seymour.

Sharp, Robert. b. 27 Sept. 1773; d. 16 June 1814.

Shaw, Elizabeth. b. 1739; d. 7 Dec. 1811; age 72 yrs.; w/o William Shaw.

Shaw, Elizabeth. b. ca. 1763; d. Nov. 1810; age 47 yrs.; w/o James Shaw.

Shaw, James. b. ca. 1762; d. 29 Mar. 1804; age 42 yrs.; h/o Elizabeth.

Shearer, Caroline. b. ca. 22 Feb. 1832; d. 13 Sept. 1834; age 2 yrs.7 mos. 23 dys.; d/o William F. & Eliza A. Shearer.

Sheftall, Benjamin. b. 26 Nov. 1830; d. 16 July 1836.

Sheftall, Caroline. b. 25 Nov. 1827; d. 1836.

Sheftall, Hannah G. b. 15 Feb. 1803; d. 10 Nov. 1834; w/o Mordecai Sheftall, Jr.

Sheftall, Lemuel Smith. b. 28 Oct. 1843; d. 2 Nov. 1844.

Shellman, John. b. ca. Jan. 1757; d. 12 May 1838; age 81 yrs. 4 mos.

Shellman, John, Jr. b. 1799; d. 9 Nov. 1821; age 22 yrs.; s/o John Shellman.

Sherlock, Ann. Native of Balbriggan Co., Dublin, Ireland; b. 1800; d. 31 Jan. 1822; age 22 yrs.; w/o James Sherlock.

Shick, George. 1849.

Simmons, John. Native of SC; b. ca. 12 Feb. 1791; d. 15 Feb. 1823; age 32 yrs. 3 dys.; left a widow.

Simpson, Rosaline Elizabeth. b. ca. 1829; d. 9 Oct. 1830; d/o William F. & Mary H. Simpson.

Simpson, William E. Native of Savannah; b. ca. 13 May 1797; d. 28 Aug. 1835; age 38 yrs.3 mos. 15 dys.

Sistare, Infant. b. 4 Apr.; d. 9 Apr. in New York.

Sistare, Julia May. b. ca. Nov. 1833; d. 28 Apr. 1837; age 4 yrs. 6 mos.; eldest d/o Horace & Lucy S. Sistare; Scarlet Fever.

Sistare, Julian Saville. b. ca. Pr. 1839; d. 8 May 1840; age 1 yr. 19 dys.; s/o Horace & Lucy S. Sistare.

Sistare, Lucy Scarbrough. b. 21 Jan. 1812; d. 29 Nov. 1840; age 28 yrs. 10 mos. 8 dys. 3rd d/o William Scarbrough; w/o Horace Sistare.

Sistare, William. b. 20 Dec. 1836; d. 5 Jan. 1837; age 15 dys.; s/o Horace & Lucy S. Sistare.

Smith, Ames. b. ca. 1794; d. 19 Nov. 1817; age 23 yrs.

Smith, Elizabeth Alice. b. 1835; d. 5 Nov. 1838; d/o Lemuel W. & Abby Smith.

Smith, Jacob. Native of New Jersey; b. 1786; d. 1820; age 35 yrs.

Smith, John. b. 1718; d. Nov. 1793; age 75 yrs.

Smith, John. Born in Ireland; b. —Feb. 1792; d. 13 Feb. 1820; emigrated to U.S. 1810.

Smith, John Cuming. Born in Newport, RI; b. ca. 24 Oct. 1834; d. 2 Sept. 1835 at Newport, RI; age 11 mos. 10 dys.; 1st s/o James and Ruth G. Smith.

Smith, Joseph. b. ca. 1822; d. 26 June 1823; age 16 mos.; s/o William & K. E. Smith.

Smith, Ruth Godfrey. b. ca. 1816; d. 28 Oct. 1836; age 20 yrs. 7 mos.; w/o James Smith; d/o George D. Sweet; m/o John Cuming Smith & infant son.

Smith, Infant son. b. 23 Oct. 1836; d. 26 Dec. 1836; s/o James & Ruth G. Smith

Smith, Virginia C. Born in Savannah. b. Jan. 1834; d. 30 Sept. 1841; age 7 yrs. 8 mos.; d/o Walter Smith.

Smith, Walter. Native of Ayrshires, Scotland; b. ca. 1784; d. 13 May 1840; age 56 yrs.

Smith, William B. b. 25 May 1836; d. 12 Nov. 1838.

Smith, William John. Native of Cavan, Ireland; b. Apr. 1823; d. 7 Jan. 1838; age 15 yrs. 9 mos.; youngest s/o James &

Elizabeth Smith; resident of Savannah several yrs.; bro/o Mary Ann Smith.

Smith, Mary Ann. b. Apr. 1823; d. 7 Jan. 1838; age 15 yrs. 9 mos.; eldest d/o James & Elizabeth Smith.

Snider, William Benjamin. b. 25 May 1836; d/ 12 Nov. 1838; s/o B. & M. T. Snider.

Spalding, James, Esq. b. ca. 1734; d. 10 Nov. 1794; age 60 yrs.

Spencer, Elizabeth. Born in England. b. ca. 1784; d. 15 Jan. 1818; age. 34 yrs.; w/o William Joseph Spencer.

Spencer, Elizabeth Gardner. b. 15 Jan. 1818; d. 21 Jan. 1818; age 6 dys.; d/o W. J. & Eliz. Spencer.

Spencer, Isabelah Jeanne. b. 4 Aug. 1813; d. 14 Aug. 1813; age 10 dys.; d/o W. J. & Eliz. Spencer. (Isabelle Jemima/ Isabella Joanna)

Spencer, Female. Stillborn 23 Aug. 1809 ; d/o W. J. & Eliz. Spencer.

Spencer, Sarah Parker. b. ca. 2 Dec. 1807; 9 Aug. 1809; age 16 mos. 7 dys. d/o W. J. & Eliz. Spencer.

Spencer, William Joseph II. b. ca. 11 Sept. 1805; d. 17 July 1806; age 10 mos. 6 dys. s/o W. J. & Eliz. Spencer.

Springer, Mrs. Margaret. b. ca. 1779; d. 22 Sept. 1845; age 65 yrs.

Starr, Marcus J. b. 16 Aug. 1830; d. 3 Oct. 1831; s/o Marcus A. & Elizabeth Starr.

Stanton, John Harvey. Infant s/o Patrick Stanton.

Stanton, Patrick. Native of Limerick, Ireland. b. ca. 1787; d. 16 July 1820; f/o John Harvey Stanton. Emigrated early in life to U.S.; Savannah merchant.

Stebbins, Benjamin. b. Apr. 1817; d. 5 Aug. 1817; age 4 mos.; s/o Edward & Catherine Stebbins.

Stebbins, Edward. b. ca. 20 Apr. 1802; d. 23 Aug. 1812; age 10 yrs. 4 mos. 3 dys.; s/o Edward & Catherine Stebbins.

Stebbins, Sarah. b. ca. 15 Mar. 1808; d. 27 July 1812; age 4 yrs. 4 mos. 12 dys.; d/o Edward & Catherine Stebbins.

Stebbins, Sarah T. b. ca. 1 Jan. 1815; d. 11 Oct. 1817; age 2 yrs. 9 mos. 11 dys.; d/o Edward & Catherine Stebbins.

Stevens, William. Born at Beaulieu, Chatham Co., GA. b. 1752; d. 6 Aug. 1819; Chief Justice of GA; Mayor of Savannah; 1st GA Attorney General.

Stewart, Charles. Native of Perth, Scotland. d. 12 Aug. 1800; bro./o James Stewart; d. on his way to New York where he had domiciliated.

Stewart, George. Native of Ireland; b. 18 Mar. 1770; d. Mar. 1815; age 36 yrs.; resided in Saint Mary's, GA 8 yrs.; mariner.

Stone, Randsom. Born in Virginia; b. ca. Dec. 1766; d. 21 Apr. 1814; age 47 yrs. 5 mos.; Cancer of the face.

Struthers, John, Esq. Of Glasgow, Scotland; b. ca. 1764; d. 24 Feb. 1790; age 26 yrs.; died on ship in Savannah River; was a Glasgow brewer; bro./o Robert Struthers of Glasgow.

Sullivan, Eugene O. Native of Parish of Killidy, Co. Kerry, Ireland; b. 1802; d. 26 Jan. 1839; age 37 yrs.

Sutcliffe, John. Native of England; b. ca. 31 May 1790; d. 26 June 1822; age 32 yrs. 27 dys.; stonecutter.

Swarbreck, Lucy C. b. 1817; d. 27 Nov. 1821; age 4 yrs.

Tatem, Joseph. b. ca. 1797; d. 30 Oct. 1820; age 23 yrs. 10 mos. 21 dys.; eldest s/o the late Joseph R. Tatem of Philadelphia, PA; apothecary; Yellow Fever.

Taylor, Catherine. b. ca. 25 Nov. 1830; d. 27 Mar. 1831; age 5 mos. 2 dys.; d/o William & Ellen Taylor.

Taylor, Jacob R., b. 1792; d. 14 Nov. 1811; age 19 yrs.; s/o John R. Taylor Philadelphia, PA. Murdered.

Taylor, John R. b. 1792; d. 14 Nov. 1811; age 19 yrs.; s/o John R. Taylor of Philadelphia, PA. Murdered.

Taylor, Samuel. b. ca. 30 Nov. 1828; d. 8 July 1830; age 1 yr. 8 mos. 9 dys.; s/o William & Ellen Taylor.

Taylor, William. Native of Castelcomer, Co. Kilkenny, Ireland; b. 1796; d. 5 June 1831; age 35 yrs.

Tebeau, Catherine Treutlen. Native of Chatham Co., GA; b. ca. 4 June 1756; d. 16 Dec. 1836; age 80 yrs. 6 mos. 12 dys.; w/o John Robert Tebeau.

Tebeau, John Robert. Native of Chatham Co., GA; b. ca. 13 Dec. 1747; d. 12 Oct. 1807; age 59 yrs. 10 mo. 25 dys. h/o Catherine Treutlen.

Tessier, Francois. Native of Pay En—Teley, France. b. 1732; d. 29 May 1818; age 86 yrs.; planter of St. Domingue. Died in Savannah.

Thomasson, Marc Honore Paul Pierre. b. 12 Oct. 1849; d. 20 May 1851; s/o Paul Francis Henri & Honore Thomasson.

Thomasson, William Francis Joseph. b. 14 Dec. 1852; d. 19 Apr. 1861; s/o Paul Francis Henri & Honore Thomasson.

Thomson, William. Native of Scotland. b. ca. 1789; d. 24 Oct. 1819; age ca. 30 yrs.

Thompson, Ann E. d. 25 July 1847.

Thompson, Edward. b. ca. Apr. 1813; d. 22 Nov. 1828; age 15 yrs. 7 mos.; b/o Emily Caroline.

Thompson, Emily Caroline.   b. ca. July 1808; d. 6 Oct. 1813; age 5 yrs. 3 mos.; sis./o Edward Thompson

Thompson, J.C. b. ca. Sept. 1789; d. 22 Feb. 1822; age 33 yrs. 5 mos.

Thompson, John. b. ca. Oct. 1792; d. 25 Feb. 1831; age 38 yrs. 4 mos.

Thompson, Marian. Of New York; b. 1800; d. 12 Oct. 1820; age 20 yrs. Yellow Fever.

Thompson, Susan Ann. b. ca. 27 Dec. 1836; d. 7 Oct. 1837; age 10 mos. 11 dys.; d/o James & Margaret Thompson.

Thompson, William. d. 13 Oct. 1811; s/o R. & Eliza Thompson.

Thompson, William H. Born in MA; b. 1808; d. 4 July 1837; age 29 yrs.

Thorp, William B. Of Providence, RI; b. ca. 1794; d. 12 Nov. 1819; age 25 yrs.

Tierney, Patrick. Native of Parish of Ballintampal, Co. Cavan, Ireland; b. 1816; d. 17 Aug. 1851; age 35 yrs.; h/o M. Tierney.

Tierney, Thomas Patrick. b. 3 Feb. 1849; d. 8 Feb. 1849; age 5 dys.; s/o Patrick & M. Tierney.

Timmons, Mary. b. 4 Dec. 1746; d. 8 Oct. 1818; age 72 yrs.

Timmons,————. Erected by his son, S. H. Timmons.

Tiot, Charles. b. ca. 1753; born in France. d. 8 June 1808; age 55 yrs.

Tiot, Helen W. b. ca. Dec. 1823; d. 5 May 1825; age 18 mos.

Tiot, Infant. d. 16 Nov. 1829; premature.

Tiot, James D. b. ca. Aug. 1828; d. 26 May 1829; age 10 mos.

Tiot, Martha Ann. b. ca. 1802; d. 18 Nov. 1833.

Tiot, Mary Ann Maria. b. ca. Aug. 1795; d. 29 Nov. 1811; age 16 yrs. 3 mos.; w/o Charles Tiot.

Tiot, Richard W. b. ca. Oct. 1825; d. 3 Sept. 1827; age 23 mos.

Tresper, Infant. Child of C. & M. A. Tresper.

Tresper, Maria E. Age 1 yr. I mos.; d/o C. & M. A. Tresper.

Tresper, Stephen B. Age 8 mos.; s/o C. & M. A. Tresper.

Trever, John. Native of Wales; b. 1736; d. 6 July 1808; age 72 yrs.; f/o Hannah Hulse; lived in Savannah ca. 40 yrs.

Trevor, Elizabeth. b. 1755; d. 10 Dec. 1797; age 42 yrs.

Trowbridge, Capt. Joseph. Of New Haven, CT.

Trushet, Charles. Native of GA. b. 1779; d. 17 Nov. 1810; age 31 yrs. Had a bro.

Trushet, Elizabeth. b. ca. Feb. 1738; d. 15 Nov. 1822; age 84 yrs. 9 mos.

Tucker, John. Native of New Jersey; b. 1777; d. 8 Jan. 1804; age 27 yrs.; drowned w/Cornelius Ludlum & Joseph White.

Tufts, Gardner. 1848.

Turnbull, Susan. Native of Providence, RI; b. 8 July 1776; d. 29 Feb. 1808; w/o Nicholas Turnbull. Left hus. & 3 young chdn.

Turner, Thomas M. b. 24 Sept. 1831; d. 19 May 1832; s/o Thomas M. & Sophia M. Turner.

Tuthill, Benjamin. b. ca. 1795; d. 12 Oct. 1820; age 25 yrs.; Yellow Fever.

Valadon, Martha Maria Georgette Bruneau. Born in St. Marc, St. Domingue; b. ca. 1749; d. 19 Sept. 1809; age 60 yrs.; w/o Monsieur Valadon.

Valleau, Mrs. Ann M. d. 10 Feb.1851; had chdn.

Vincent, Thomas. b. ca. 1728; d. Sept. 1767.

Vickers, Dr. Samuel. Born in New Brunswick, NJ.; b. 1755; d. 15 Oct. 1785; Honors at Princeton Coll. NJ.; had bro. T.L.Vickers.

Wade, Isabella Julia. b. 29 Nov. 1831; d. 10 Nov. 1836; d/o James H. & Eleanor M. Wade.

Waldron, Martha C. b. ca. 20 July 1812; d. 31 Aug. 1838; age 36 yrs. 2 mos. 11 dys.

Wallace, James. b. ca. 1754; d. 21 Jan. 1825; age 71 yrs. Late His Brittannic Majesty's Consul for the State of GA.

Wallace, John. b. ca. 1750; d. 11 Sept. 1804; age 54 yrs.

Wallace, John. b. ca. 1795; d. 13 May 1816; age 21 yrs.

Wallace, Margaret. b. ca. 1795; d. 29 Nov. 1827; age 32 yrs.

Wallace, Mary. b. 30 July 1766; d. 31 Dec. 1852; age 87 yrs.; wid./o John Wallace. Large family.

Wallace, Sarah. b. 21 Nov. 1798; d. 29 Sept. 1802.

Wallen, Jane M. b. 30 June 1815; d. 20 Sept. 1816; d/o E. & Jane Ann Wallen.

Walter, George A. Native of Providence, RI; b. 1792; d. 7 Oct. 1817; age 25 yrs.

Ward, John Elliott. b. 7 Aug. 1842; d. 28 Mar. 1850; 2nd s/o John E. & Olivia B. Ward.

Ward, Hall McAllister. b. 9 Jan. 1843; d. 23 June 1845; 3rd s/o John E. & Olivia B. Ward.

Ward, William Gordon. b. 9 Oct. 1846; d. 6 July 1857; 4th s/o John E. & Olivia B. Ward.

Warner, Joseph S. Of Providence, RI; b. 1792; d. 27 Aug. 1813; age 21 yrs.

Warner, Moses. Of Pittsfield, MA; b. 1792; d. 27 Dec. 1819; age 27 yrs.; s/o Joseph Warner of Northampton, MA.

Warren, Andrew J. Born in GA; b. ca. May 1830; d. 14 Oct. 1833; age 3 yrs. 5 mos.; s/o Robert B. Warren.

Warren, Robert B. Born in GA; b. 1810; d. 18 Apr. 1834; age 24 yrs.; f/o Andrew J. & Sarah Warren.

Warren, Sarah. b. ca. Dec. 1831; d. 24 Sept. 1833; age 21 mos.; d/o Robert B. Warren.

Warrington, William. Native of Boston, MA; b. ca. Jan. 1770; d. 8 Oct. 1803; age 33 yrs. 9 mos.; left widow.

Watson, Harriet D. b. ca. 28 June 1826; d. 4 July 1829; age 3 yrs. 7 dys.

Watt, Alexander. b. 1754; d. 10 Nov. 1801; age 47 yrs.; resident of Sav. many yrs.; h/o Ann.

Watt, Ann. b. 1770; d. 14 Jan. 1834; age 64 yrs.; wid./o Alexander Watt. Had chdn.

Watts, Anna. b. 1773; d. 13 July 1796; age 23 yrs.; w/o Robert Watts of Savannah; d/o Thomas Hopkins, Esq. of Hartford, CT.

Watts, Leleah Heriot. b. 1788; d. 16 Sept. 1815; age 27 yrs.; w/o Robert Watts.

Waudin, John William. d. 25 Sept. 1794; apprentice to John Cunningham, merchant in Savannah.

Wayne, Richard Pawson. b. ca. June 1787; d. 29 Aug. 1795; age 8 yrs. 2 mos.; s/o Richard & Elizabeth Wayne. ?

Webb, Ann M. b. 1806; d. 19 Nov. 1834.

Webb, Mary. b. ca. Nov. 1834; d. 27 May 1837; age 2 yrs. 6 mos.; d/o Amos & Caroline Webb.

Weitman, Matthew. b. Sept. 1795; d. 8 June 1837.

Welch, Miss Ann. Born in Ireland; b. Jan. 1799; d. 3 Oct. 1819; age 20 yrs. 9 mos.

Welch, Mrs. Nancy. b. 1817; d. 7 June 1845; age 28 yrs.

Wells, James. From Hartford, CT; b. 1797; d. 8 Nov. 1830; age 33 yrs. Blacksmith.

Welman, Ruth. Born in Savannah; b. ca. 1785; d. 5 Mar. 1822.

White, Mr. Edward. Of Haverhill, MA; b. 1783; d. 4 July 1808; age 25 yrs.

White, Maj. Edward. Born in Brooklyn, MA; b. 1758; d. 9 Jan. 1812; age 54 yrs.; Officer of Rev. Army.

White, Eugene Augustus Theodotus. b. ca. May 1821; d. 21 Oct. 1830; age 9 yrs. 5 mos.; s/o George & Elizabeth White.

White, Joseph. Native of New Jersey; b. 1775; d. 8 Jan. 1804; age 32 yrs.   Drowned w/John Tucker & Cornelius Ludlum.

White, Melancton L. Born in NY; b. ca. 1795; d. 18 Nov. 1819; had a brother.

Whitel, Richard. Age 58 yrs.

Whittendel, Mrs. Elizabeth. b. 1775; d. 26 Apr. 1800; age 25 yrs.; w/o John T. Whittendel; d/o Capt. Gilbert Harrison.

Wier, Mrs. Rachel. Native of Middletown, NJ; b. 1773; d. 20 Dec. 1826; age 53 yrs.; resided in N.Providence, Nassau, for 44 yrs.; left hus. & 7 chdn.

Wilde, James, Esq. Born in Baltimore, MD; b. 1793; d. 16 Jan. 1815; age 22 yrs.; late Paymaster in U.S. Army; died in duel.

Wilder, Joseph Washburn. Of Leicester, MA; b. ca. 1817; d. 12 Oct. 1841; age 24 yrs.; 2nd s/o John Wilder.

Williams, Ann. Native of Battle Hill, NJ; b. 1774; d. 23 Sept. 1827; age 53 yrs.

Williams, Daniel. b. ca. 2 June 1801; d. 27 Aug. 1803; age 2 yrs. 2 mos. 25 dys.; s/o Richard & Amy Williams.

Williams, Feriby. b. 1774; d. 13 Oct. 1804; age 30 yrs.; w/o John Williams.

Williams, Louisa B. b. ca. Mar. 1796; d. 13 June 1800; age 4 yrs. 3 mos.; d/o John & Feriby Williams.

Williams, Maria. Born in Savannah; b. ca. 2 Apr. 1813; d. 4 Sept. 1833; age 20 yrs. 5 mos. 2 dys.; d/o Wm. T. & Harriet C. Williams.

Williams, Mrs. Maria. Born in London, England. b. 20 Dec. 1748; d. 11 Dec. 1833, Savannah, GA; age 85 yrs.; wid./o James Williams; d/o William Thorne.

Williams, Nathan Jr. Of Tolland, CT; b. 1760; d. 16 Dec. 1784; age 24 yrs.

Williams, Nathaniel. b. ca. July 1803; d. 12 Aug. 1804; age 11 mos.; s/o Richard & Amy Williams.

Williams, Nathaniel. b. 1787; d. 18 Oct. 1803; age 16 yrs.

Williams, Nathaniel, Sr. b. 1753; d. 27 June 1803; age 50 yrs.

Williamson, Bennett. b. ca. 9 May 1815; d. 27 Aug. 1836; age 21 yrs. 3 mos. 18 dys.

Williamson, William Bower. b. 1728; d. Feb. 1762; age 34 yrs.

Wilson, Collier G. A. b. ca. 1837; d. 15 May 1838; d/o T. A. & E. Wilson.

Wilson, Daniel Stewart Lafayette. b. ca. 1825; d. 22 Sept. 1833; age 8 yrs.; s/o J. G. & J. Dennis Wilson.

Wilson, Jane Dennis. d. 13 Nov. 1847; w/o J. G. Wilson.

Wilson, Mary Madeline Dennis. b. ca. 1822; d. 1 June 1837; age 15 yrs.; d/o J. G. & J. Dennis Wilson.

Wilson, Richard Dennis Stiles. b. ca. 1824; d. 28 June 1847; age 23 yrs.; s/o J. G. & J. Dennis Wilson.

Wilson, Peyton Lisbey Wade. b. ca. 1829; d. 1 Oct. 1835; age 6 yrs.; s/o J. G. & J. Dennis Wilson.

Wilson, William. b. ca. 1774; d. 29 Sept. 1807; age 33 yrs.

Winkler, Anne M. b. ca. 5 Sept. 1805; d. 12 Aug. 1825; age 19 yrs. 11 mo. 7 dys.; w/o Z. M. Winkler; left 2 infant babes.

Winn, Mrs. Jane. b. 1754; d. 29 Aug. 1816; age 62 yrs.; m/o Thomas Winn; left a large family.

Wise, Serene. Born in Savannah; b. ca. 1804; d. 24 Oct. 1807; age 3 yrs.; d/o Stephen Wise.

Witham, Charles. Born in Norfolk, VA; b. ca. Apr. 1802; d. 9 Nov. 1806; age 3 yrs. 7 mos.; only surviving chd/o James & Mary Witham.

Witham, Mrs. Mary. b. 1781; d. 2 July 1806; age 25 yrs.; w/o Capt. James Witham.

Withington, Mrs. Martha W. Native of Charleston, SC; b. 1814; d. 11 Oct. 1844; age 30 yrs.; survived by hus.

Wood, Ellen. Born in Scotland; b. 1806; d. 3 Nov. 1841.

Wood, Ezekiel. Native of Upton, MA. b. ca. 29 May 1792; d. 8 Dec. 1832; age 40 yrs., 7 mos. 10 dys. Merchant in Savannah for last 16 yrs.

Wood, Ezekiel G. b. ca. 13 Nov. 1832; d. 26 Feb. 1833; age 3 mos. 12 dys.; s/o Ezekiel & Susan Wood.

Wood, Mary Goodell. d. 4 June 1831; d/o Ezekiel & Susan Wood.

Woodbridge, William. Born in Salem, Mass.; b. 10 Feb. 1780; d. 21 Aug. 1820, Savannah; s/o Dudley & Dorcas Woodbridge; yellow fever.

Woodruff, Harriot. b. 1776; d. 10 Dec. 1808; age 32 yrs.; w/o Abner Woodruff.

Woodruff, Isreal. Of New York City; born in Elizabethtown, NJ; b. 1780. d. 2 Sept. 1812.

Woodruff, Luther. Of New York City; b. 1790; d. 4 Sept. 1823.

Woolhopter, Elizabeth M. Infant; b. ca. 1811; d. 1813; age 14 mos.; d/o Philip D. Woolhopter.

Woolhopter, Philip D. Born in NY; b. 1769; d. 11 Feb. 1818; age 49 yrs.; f/o Elizabeth & Sarah Ann.

Woolhopter, Sarah Ann. Infant. b. 1810; d. 1810; age 10 mos. 27 dys.; d/o Philip D. Woolhopter.

Worthington, Capt. Peter. Native of Liverpool, England. b. ca. 1776; d. 23 Nov. 1811; age 35 yrs.; left wife & chdn.

Wrist, Levi. b. ca. 1784; d. 23 Feb. 1819; age 35 yrs.

Young, Mrs. Eliza Ruth. b. ca. 1730; d. 18 June 1814; age 86 yrs.; wid./o Thomas Young, Esq.

Young, Elizabeth. b. 17 Dec. 1770; d. 5 May 1804.

Young, John C.   Native of Ridpath, Shire of Roxbury, Taredale County, Scotland; b. ca. 1786; d. 11 Sept. 1817; age 31 yrs.; left wife & chdn.

Young, Thomas.   Native of Scotland; b. ca. 1752; d. 7 Nov. 1808; age 56 yrs.

Young, Thomas, Esq.   b. ca. 1777; d. 6 Aug. 1832; age 55 yrs.

Young, William.   Born in Scotchtown, Orange Co., NY; b. 1791; d. 12 Feb. 1811.

Zebly, Sarah.   b. 7 June 1786; d. 23 Sept. 1820. age 34 yrs. 3 mos. 16 dys.; w/o Joseph P. Zebley of Philadelphia, PA.

ABBREVIATIONS

aft.	After	neph/o	Nephew of
b.	Born	prop.	Proprietor
bef.	Before	sl/o	Sister- in- law of
bro.	Brother	sis.	Sister
ca.	Circa; about	sis/o	Sister of
chd.	Child	s/o	Son of
chdn.	Children	unc./o	Uncle of
d.	Died	w/o	Wife of
dau.	Daughter	wid.	Widow
d/o	Daughter of	wks.	Weeks
dys.	Days	yrs.	Years
f/o	Father of		
gr.d.o	Granddaughter of		
h/o	Husband of		
hus.	Husband		
inf.	Infant		
m/o	Mother of		
mos.	Months		

NOTE: Unless indicated otherwise, these individuals died in Savannah, GA.

COLONIAL CEMETERY TRIVIA
FACTS AND MYTHS

1. There were originally between 8,000 and 11,00 burials, of which only about 600 are identified by a marker.

2. There are fifty large brick family vaults remaining in the cemetery. There were once many more, but they have either been destroyed or removed to Laurel Grove or Bonaventure cemeteries.

3. Two more rows of graves probably extend past the fence on Abercorn Street.

4. James Poince, an engineer who died in 1849, was accidentally shot by his best friend while on board a ship in the Savannah River.

5. The oldest marked grave is that of William Bowers Williamson who died in 1762.

6. The oldest person buried here is Marie Elizabeth Malaurie who died in 1842 at the age of 93 years. She was a native of France, and her epitaph is written in French.

7. The oldest man buried in Colonial Cemetery is Francois Tessier who died in 1818 at the age of 86 years. The cause of his death was attributed to "old age".

8. Some of the gnarled crepe myrtle trees are over a hundred years old.

9. Some people who were buried in Colonial Cemetery, and later moved to Laurel Grove, were also moved again later to Bonaventure, thus moving more times after death than they probably did when they were alive.

10. George Washington is believed to have contributed money toward building the brick wall around the cemetery in 1791. The only remaining part of this wall is on the east side of the cemetery.

11. The Spanish moss on the trees is an epiphyte, not a parasite. It does not kill the trees.

12. There are no documented ghosts associated with Colonial Cemetery. Perhaps all the moving and removing of bodies thoroughly disoriented them, and they remain safely interred.

13. Some of General Sherman's men lived in some of the large family vaults in 1864.

14. One of the stones, that of Amie Arnold who died in 1872, came from another cemetery. She is not buried here, nor have I found any record of her at Laurel Grove or at Bonaventure.

15. The government-issued stone engraved with the name Joseph Brown who died in 1945 probably came here from another cemetery and does not actually mark a grave.

16. Two famous people who may lie here in unmarked graves are Peter Tondee and Dr. Mary Lavinder.

17. There is believed to be at least one mass grave of 1820 yellow fever victims in the southern section of the cemetery.

18. The greatest number of burials in any one year occurred in 1820, with most of them taking place in October, followed by September and November.

19. There are approximately sixty-five marked graves that date in the 1700's.

20. The longest epitaph is either that of Mrs. Caroline Lloyd who was less than 18 years old when she died in 1830, or that of Sarah Norris Hill, on the east wall. You be the judge.

21. The epitaph on the stone of John Struthers, Esq., was written by his brother, Robert Struthers, and gives a brief biography as well as an advertisement of his Glasgow Brewery which Robert inherited.

22. The historical marker to William Stevens does not mark an actual grave site. Stevens, who was born in 1752 at Beaulieu, was a Chief Justice of Georgia and also Mayor of Savannah. He was the first Georgia Attorney General. He died August 6, 1819.

23. The marble headstone of Richard Julia S. Pinto, oldest son of Gaston Puito Silva of Madeira, is engraved in both Portuguese and in English. He died in 1818. The stone is fastened on the east wall.

24. Sir Patrick Houston and Lady Houston were both interred in Colonial Cemetery, but were later moved to Bonaventure Cemetery.

25. Five governors of Georgia are buried here: James Habersham, Archibald Bulloch, Samuel Elbert, Button Gwinnett, and Richard Howley.

26. One of the framers of the Constitution of the United States, William Leigh Pierce, lies in Colonial Cemetery in a grave whose stone was destroyed by vandals and whose location is therefore unknown.

27. There are literally thousands of unmarked graves scattered throughout the cemetery.

28. None of the early maps of the city that I examined show the cemetery extending past the Abercorn Street line. In the 1770's there were many burials scattered throughout the city prompting the council to forbid burials anywhere in the city, other than the designated burial ground.

29. The majority of the graves in Colonial Cemetery are oriented on an east-west line, with the stone's face toward the east. This custom was based on the idea of the resurrection of the dead occurring with the rising sun in the east. The dead were, therefore, interred facing east to await judgment day.

30. The large slabs or tablets which lie flush with the ground were originally raised on pillars or piers, and are sometimes the covers for underground vaults. The large vaults are unique to Savannah and Charleston. A few may be found scattered throughout the low country.

EIGHTEENTH CENTURY BURIALS

1. 1762 — William Bower Williamson
2. 1763 — Mary Bolton Habersham
3. 1763 — George Cuthbert
4. 1766 — Mary Bryan

5. 1767 — Thomas Vincent, Esq.

6. 1768 — George Cuthbert, Esq.

7. 1769 — James Johnston

8. 1770 — Theodora Ash

9. 1771 — Rev. Samuel Frink

10. 1772 — Telamon Cuyler

11. 1773 — John Dieterick Schaeffer

12. 1775 — James Habersham

13. 1776 — Noah W. Bradley

14. 1777 — Button Gwinnett

15. 1777 — Archibald Bulloch

16 1778 — John Dieterich Schaeffer

17. 1779 — Col. John Maitland

18. 1782 — Capt. John Christie

19. 1783 — Mary Elizabeth Demere

20. 1783 — Edward Augustus Boulineau

21. 1784 — Nathaniel Williams, Jr.

22. 1784 — Richard Howley

23. 1785 — Dr. Samuel Vickers

24. 1785 — Mrs. Sarah Schick

25. 1786 — Nathanael Greene

26. 1786 — James Storie

27. 1787 — Henry Hodgson

28. 1788 — Samuel Elbert*

29. 1789 — Robert Bolton

30. 1789 — William Leigh Pierce

31. 1790 — Frederick Herb

32. 1790 — John Struthers, Esq.

33. 1790 — Hannah Morel

34. 1790 — Elizabeth Cunningham Cuyler

35. 1790 — Jane Russell

36. 1790 — Sally Ross

37. 1791 — Sarah W. Leggett

38. 1791 — Rebecca Harriett Pinder

39. 1791 — Mrs. Lillibridge

40. 1792 — Elizabeth Rae Elbert*

41. 1792 — Joseph Ottolenghe, Esq.
42. 1793 — Miss Maria Stiles
43. 1793 — John Fisher Drinker
44. 1793 — Grace Carr Belcher
45. 1793 — James Pryce Belcher
46. 1793 — John Smith
47. 1793 — George Washington Greene
48. 1794 — James Spalding
49. 1794 — John William Waudin
50. 1794 — John C. Belcher
51. 1794 — William Thomson
52. 1795 — Rev. Edward Ellington
53. 1795 — Thomas Pawson Wayne
54. 1795 — Richard Randolph
55. 1795 — James Whitfield, Esq.
56. 1795 — Gabriel Leaver
57. 1796 — Mrs. Martha Whitfield
58. 1796 — Anna Watts
59. 1796 — Titus Powers
60. 1796 — Anne Guerard
61. 1796 — Mrs. Elizabeth Whitefield
62. 1797 — Capt. Jeremiah Dickinson
63. 1797 — Elizabeth Trevor
64. 1797 — Capt. John Moore, Esq.
65. 1797 — John Schick
66. 1797 — Robert Moriah Forsyth
67. 1798 — Stephen F. Randolph
68. 1799 — John Currie, Esq.
69. 1799 — Bethiah Neckerson

* Interred in 1924

KNOWN STONE CUTTERS
IN COLONIAL CEMETERY

The stone cutters or stone masons listed here were taken directly from the stones which they either signed or which had characteristic marks or traits belonging to them:

      Robert Allen
      Andrew Gow — Savannah
      J. Gow — Savannah
      J. White — Savannah
      Walker — Savannah
  ? D. Fillas — New Haven, CT
      E. A. Price, Sr. —
      Arthur Smith — ?
      James Coleman — Savannah
      (Originally from Newark, New Jersey)
      Robert Jones — Savannah
      John Bull — Connecticut
      T. Cooley — Providence, Rhode Island
      D. Ritter — New Haven, CT
      Moore & Lyman — Savannah
      Caleb————
      W. A.——————
      William Masterton
      John Sutcliffe

There were likely other stone cutters working in Savannah, but these are the ones whose names were on the stones I examined. The names of Andrew Gow, James Coleman, and Moore & Lyman appeared most frequently.

Four of these stonecutters are buried in Colonial Cemetery, but there are stones for only three. Robert Jones, age 15, was a stonecutter who died in 1820 of yellow fever. His grave is not marked. The other three which do have grave markers are William Masterton, John Sutcliffe, and Sumner Moore.

Tombstone of Sumner Moore

CEMETERY GLOSSARY AND SYMBOLISM

As the visitor to the cemetery strolls along its paths and reads the epitaphs, he will encounter certain expressions and wording that may be unfamiliar, strange, or unusual. The following explanations may be helpful.

BRAIN FEVER: Encephalitis.

CONSORT : A spouse; generally used to denote a wife who died before her husband.

CONSUMPTION: A medical term given as a cause of death from tuberculosis.

EPITAPH: The inscription on a grave marker. It includes the person's name, birth date, death date, sometimes the age of the person, and sometimes the cause of death. It often includes poems, Bible verses, or tributes to the person's life. It may include an f, the symbol that resembles an f, found within certain words, which is in reality an old English way of writing an S.

RELICT: Usually used to signify that the woman was a widow. I have not found this on a man's grave.

R.I.P./REQUIESCAT IN PACE: A blessing meaning, "Rest in peace."

While there is not a great deal of early American funeral art depicted on the early stones, a few of them do show carvings that are fine, frequently found in abundance in other sections of the country.

There are some carvings of funerary symbolism to be found on many of the later stones. All of the commonly used gravestone symbols are not represented in this list. I have included only those which may be found on the stones and markers in Colonial Cemetery.

A close-up view of the rattlesnake carved on the Archibald Bulloch monument.
Photo by Stacey Yongue

The beautifully carved urn on top of the Joseph Clay monument.
Photo by Stacey Yongue

BAT: This figure symbolizes the night or darkness of death.

BROKEN COLUMN: A life broken or cut short is reprsented by this symbol.

CIRCLES: Circles denote eternity.

CROSSES: There are several different types of crosses to be found in Colonial Cemetery, but they all represent the Christian faith, Resurrenction.

CROWN: A crown symbolizes that one has attained the crown of eternal life.

DEATH'S HEAD: Referred to by many as a skull and cross-bones, this represents the mortality of the person, a reminder that all become dust. This is a 17th or early 18th century device.

DRAPES: These are portrayed in various ways, but suggest the draped coffin, or the drapes of formal mourning dress. The drawing or closing of drapes signifies the closing of life.

HOURGLASS: This symbol reminds one that life, like time, runs out. It represents one's life has run its course.

LILIES: Lilies have long been associated with death and mourning; represent purity and innocence .

MASONIC EMBLEMS: Obviously these show that the person was a follower of Freemasonry.

POPPIES: These flowers symbolize the sleep of death. They have their origin in the opium poppies which induce forgetfulness and sleep.

SCROLL: This symbol represents the account of the person's life on earth.

SCYTHE: This implement, used to cut grain, symbolizes a life cut off or severed.

SERPENT: The serpent is a symbol of knowledge or wisdom.

SUNBURST FIGURES: These probably indicate that the person has passed on to a brighter glory.

THISTLE: This is a Scottish emblem which is used as a token of remembrance.

TREE STUMPS or BROKEN TREES: These are symbols for a life cut short by death.

URNS: These are generally classical in appearance, and represent the urns used in cremation. They represent the death of the human body. They usually date the stone as either late 18th or early 19th century.

VINES: These generally have a Biblical significance.

WEEPING WILLOWS: These are a traditional symbol of mourning. Some are very realistically executed, while others are stylized. A few seem more like low country trees draped in the familiar Spanish moss.

WREATHS: Quite often these are laurel wreaths which are used to honor someone.

WINGED SOUL: This symbol is used to depict the soul being freed from its earthly body and flying away to its Creator. When such a carving has personal touches, such as a wig, it is called a SOUL PORTRAIT. These are generally found on mid-18th century stones.

CHRONOLOGY OF COLONIAL CEMETERY

1750 — Established as the second public burial ground in Savannah.

1758 — Christ Episcopal Church acquires ownership of the cemetery.

1763 — Burial ground extended to Abercorn Street line and also southward.

1773-1782 — British troops quarter horses and men in cemetery.

1768 — Further enlargement of burial ground.

1783 — Citizens seek funds to rebuild the wall destroyed by British troops.

1789 — Burial ground enlarged east and south, making a total size of 500 square feet.

1791— Funds solicited to build a brick wall around the site; indications that George Washington, on his visit to Savannah, may have made a contribution.

1820 — Great yellow fever epidemic — more than 700 citizens died in the city — mass burials occurred.

1849 — Evergreen-Bonaventure Cemetery established.

1853 — Laurel Grove and Catholic Cemeteries established; 160 burials moved to Catholic and to Evergreen - Bonaventure.

1853 — The Old Cemetery closed to public burials; city offered free removal and re-interment in Laurel Grove Cemetery; approximately 600 individual burials removed from Colonial Cemetery and re-interred.

1864 — Union forces occupy Savannah and quarter men, heavy artillery, and horses in the cemetery.

1868 — Old Cemetery Association formed to attempt preservation of the site — first preservation attempt.

1887 — The Georgia Historical Society attempts to map and record the markers in the old cemetery.

1896 — The old brick wall is torn down, misplaced and damaged stones are placed on east wall.

1897 — Cemetery is sold to the city, with certain restricting covenants — Park and Tree Commision embarks on project to clean and beautify the site.

1902 — General Nathanael Greene's remains are removed from the Graham vault and placed under the monument on Johnson Square.

1913 — The Daughters of the American Revolution erect the arched gate at the northeast entrance in honor of the American Revolutionary soldiers buried in the cemetery.

1922 — Legal battles ensue when the city attempts to extend Lincoln Street from Perry Lane to Oglethorpe Avenue.

1924 — The Colonial Dames of Georgia copy and publish the epitaphs on the markers in a publication, *Some Early Epitaphs in Georgia.* The remains of Samuel Elbert, an early governor of Georgia, and those of his wife are removed from their plantation, Rae's Hall, and re-interred with honors in Colonial Park Cemetery.

1935 — FERA [Federal Emergency Relief Act] of Savannah, along with Savannah Historical Research Association, make a survey and documentation of markers.

1945 — (?)A special burial is permitted for Private Joseph Brown(?). Rampant vandalism is prevalent.

1956 — The city erects a wrought iron railing around three sides of the cemetery.

1966 — The Trustees' Garden Club begins restoration, and sprinklers, lights, tabby walks, and trash receptacles are placed in the cemetery.

1967 — During road work on Abercorn Street, three skeletons are discovered three and a half feet below the surface. These are re-interred in the southeast corner of the cemetery. A plain concrete post is erected over the site.

1980's — More vandalism; archaeological survey made by

Armstrong College of Savannah.

1990's — Current preservation efforts begin, and are under-way.

EXCEPTIONS MADE ON INTERMENTS AFTER 1853

Although the cemetery was officially closed to interments in July, 1853, there were some exceptions made, and later interments allowed. Known interments after 1853 are as follows:

1. 1861 — The remains of William Francais Josef Thomasson added to the tomb of his brother, Marc Honore Paul Pierre Thomasson.

2. 1901 — Major General Nathanael Greene's remains removed from Graham vault and re-interred in Johnson Square, along with those of his son.

3. 1924 — Remains of Samuel Elbert, an early Governor of Georgia, and those of his wife removed from his plantation, Rae's Hall, and re-interred with honors in Colonial Cemetery. His original burial site was threatened by development of the property.

4. 1945 — (?)Private Joseph Brown. There is little information about this particular burial, but most sources seem to indicate the stone was removed from another location and   placed here.

5. 1967—Three skeletons are discovered during the course of some roadwork on Abercorn. They were re-interred in the southeast corner and are marked by a plain, unmarked concrete post.

Although the site was officially closed to burials on July 1, 1853, it is highly likely that there were other interments in the family tombs that already existed. For example, the family vault of Benjamin Burroughs has a date of 1857 inscribed on it.

AUTHOR'S COMMENTS

Colonial Park Cemetery is a unique site in that it contains the essence of the history of Savannah and of Georgia in a way that is not found in other cemeteries of this type.

The sheer number of historically significant burials, the diversity of people, the rich sea-faring traditions, and the mystique evoked by the unmarked burials all lend themselves to establishing a sense of the colorful fabric which is Savannah. These were real people with real desires and real accomplishments. They established businesses, they raised families, they dealt with disease and human weaknesses. Many of them left the familiar life in another land to come to a place that no doubt was an unknown integer to become a citizen in a new land, with new problems and new demands.

These were people who had faced famine, religious persecution, political dissension, and failure in their native lands, and were now presented with an opportunity to create a different life for themselves. They brought their own varied languages, beliefs, customs, and convictions, and wove them on the loom of a new world in which the individual was master of his fate.

Often there were failures. Death was the equalizing factor that too frequently quelled the ambition and the hope of aristocrat and laborer alike. But, just as disease, or accident, or even murder, could abruptly halt the best-laid plans and dreams, so, too, could these ambitions be realized with astounding success.

This perseverance is evident today as one compares the names of the dead who rest here with the same names that survive in everyday usage. Few of us think of these people as we travel the streets of Savannah that bear their names — Habersham, Bolton,

LaRoche, Gwinnett, Lathrop, Battey, Gaston, and others. But they are here. All of them — Forsyth, Cuyler, Burroughs, and Screven — lie here beneath the oaks.

To those of us who were fortunate enough to have been born and bred Southerners, the past is always with us. We tend to look upon our ancestors as never having left this plane of existence. It is our inclination to regard them as still looking over our shoulders as we pursue our mundane concerns. They hover eternally in some ethereal realm. We are comfortable with our ghosts. We speak of them as if we knew them intimately, and as if it were only yesterday that they left us. We are haunted by their legacy, good or not so good, and they unconsciously mold our own beliefs and actions, and give meaning to our way of life. They are not saints, nor are they dreadful sinners. Their bones rest here, and although it is not for us to judge, we should take pride in the tapestry they wove. Their errors give us a guide by which we learn, and their accomplishments set a standard for us to achieve.

Walk here a while and contemplate the dead. See them as the threads that bind our lives.

Honor them as people just like us. They mourned their children and their loved ones just as we.

No flowers deck their lonely graves, nor do monuments proclaim many of their resting places. Some of them made a place for themselves in history books. Some were heroic, and some were infamous. Most were just ordinary, everyday people. But they are here, and so are we. Walk with them a while and hear their stories. Tread softly and do not disturb their sleep. Honor their memory. They remain an indelible part of our lives.

- ELIZABETH CARPENTER PIECHOCINSKI

EARLY PHOTOGRAPHS AND POSTCARDS
OF COLONIAL PARK CEMETERY

The following photographs show before and after views of the 1897 beautification program initiated by the Park and Tree Commission. As is evident from the photographs taken in 1896, the cemetery was overgrown with weeds and the monuments were in a dilapidated condition. Many were crumbling, and some had completely fallen to the ground. Several of the vaults stood open to the elements. The brick wall that once surrounded the entire cemetery is also visible.

The 1897 photographs, taken after the project was completed, show a pleasant park-like atmosphere. However, it is obvious that stones were pulled up and removed to create pathways. The brick wall was removed, leaving the site open on three sides. Some of the box tombs were either filled in by surrounding soil or were lowered to almost ground level. Other monuments appear to have been removed or relocated. The plantings were part of the beautification program.

While the intentions of the beautification program were to clean up and improve the site, it is quite apparent today that these efforts were a sort of legalized vandalism as much valuable information was destroyed in the process. The walkways created at this time were constructed over grave sites, and the stones removed. Some of the stones were preserved by being placed on the east wall, but doubtless, many others were discarded.

These photographs were taken January 21, 1896, before restoration, and again on November 21, 1897, after restoration was completed.

View 1. This is Colonial Park from fifty feet north of the Abercorn Street gate, looking east. It was taken in 1896. Note the large number of monuments, the brick wall, and the old brick vaults. Courtesy Georgia Historical Society.

View 2. This is roughly the same view taken after the restoration in 1897. A paved walk has been laid, new plantings added, and some of the stones removed. Courtesy Georgia Historical Society.

View 3. This 1896 view of Colonial Park is taken from the northwest corner, looking southeast. Notice the large brick vault on the left is open. Part of the brick wall that surrounded the cemetery is visible on the right. Also note the large number of vaults and box tombs. Courtesy Georgia Historical Society.

View 4. This is almost the same view, but was taken in 1897. The large brick vault is gone, as are some of the others. The wall has been removed and Abercorn Street is now visible. Many of the stones are no longer there. The cathedral is visible in the background. Courtesy Georgia Historical Society.

View 5. This 1896 view is from in front of the Tufts vault, looking south. The poor condition of some of the vaults is evident. The portion of the brick wall along Perry Lane is clearly visible. Note the box tombs on the right. Courtesy Georgia Historical Society.

View 6. This November 21, 1897, photograph was also taken from in front of the Tufts vault, looking south and showing a new walkway and newly-installed bench, as well as new landscaping. The Cathedral is clearly visible in the distance. The brick wall is still in evidence along Perry Lane, as are a number of the buildings that back onto the lane. Note how the box tombs have been lowered. Courtesy Georgia Historical Society.

View 7. This photograph, taken in January 1896 by J. N. Wilson, shows the
derelict condition of the Graham vault as well as others. The gate on the right is
the Lincoln Street entrance from Oglethorpe Avenue. Note the brick wall.
Courtesy Georgia Historical Society.

View 8. This view of the cemetery was taken from the Lincoln Street entrance
on Ogelthorpe Avenue, looking west. "Big Duke" is visible, as is Independent
Presbyterian Church. Photographed by M. E. Wilson, November 1897.
Courtesy Georgia Historical Society.

View 9. In this photograph, showing the vaults which stood near the
Lincoln Street entrance on Oglethorpe Avenue, the table tomb of
Eliza Berrien is clearly visible. The large white vault between the Tiot
and Jones vaults is no longer there. The Graham vault is visible near
the left side of the picture. The large brick vault between the
Graham and Wylly vaults is also missing. Date of photograph
unknown, but prior to 1896. Courtesy Georgia Historical Society.

View 10. Circa late 1890's, this view is to the west from the duellist's grave, look-
ing toward Abercorn Street and Oglethorpe Avenue. The vault on the left is the
Scarbrough vault. A fire watchtower is visible behind the old firehouse. Courtesy
Georgia Historical Society.

View 11. This postcard from the early 1900's is a view of Colonial Cemetery looking east on Oglethorpe Avenue toward the police barracks. Note that there is no fence around the cemetery. From the Eric Wooddell collection.

View 12. This postcard, c. 1925, gives a bird's eye view of the cemetery toward the west. The large brick building in the upper left is the DeRenne Apartments on Liberty Street. On the far right, "Big Duke" and Independent Presbyterian Church are visible, as is Chatham Academy. From the Eric Wooddell collection.

BIBLIOGRAPHY

Books

1. Abercrombie, T. F., M.D. *History of Public Health in Georgia, 1733-1950.* Atlanta: Georgia Department of Public Health.

2. *A History of the City Government of Savannah, Ga., from 1790 to 1901.* Compiled from Official Records by Thomas Gamble, Jr., Secretary to the Mayor, Under Direction of the City Council, 1900.

3. *Annals of Georgia, Chatham County Mortuary Records.* Compiled by Caroline Price Wilson.

4. Barrow, Elfrida DeRenne, and Bell, Laura Palmer. *Anchored Yesterdays.* Savannah. Review Publishing Company, 1923.

5. Braynard, Frank O. *S.S. Savannah: The Elegant Steam Ship.* Athens, Georgia. University of Georgia Press, 1963.

6. Caldwell, Joseph, and McCann, Catherine. *Irene Mound Site, Chatham County, Georgia.* Athens. University of Georgia Press, 1941.

7. Clemens, William Montgomery. *Button Gwinnett, Man of Mystery.* Pompton Lakes, New Jersey. William M. Clemens, Publisher, 1921.

8. Combs, Diana Williams. *Early Gravestone Art in Georgia and South Carolina.* Athens. University of Georgia Press, 1986.

9. Debolt, Margaret Wayt. *Savannah: A Historical Portrait.* Spartanburg. Donning Company, Publishers, 1974.

10. *Early Deaths in Savannah, Georgia, 1763-1803: Obituaries and Legal Notices.* Compiled by the Genealogical Committee of the Georgia Historical Society, Savannah, 1989.

11. Fancher, Betsy. Savannah: *A Renaissance of the Heart*. Garden City, New York. Doubleday & Company, 1976.

12. Freeman, Ron. *Savannah People, Places and Events*. Savannah. H. Ronald Freeman, Publisher, 1997.

13. Gamble, Thomas. *Savannah Duels and Duelists. 1773-1877*. Spartanburg. The Reprint Company, Publishers, 1974.

14. Gay, Evelyn Ward. *The Medical Profession in Georgia, 1733-1983*. 1983.

15. Gillon, Edmund Vincent, Jr. *Early New England Gravestone Rubbings*. New York. Dover Publications, Inc., 1966.

16. Godly, Margaret, and Lillian C. Bragg. *Savannah Anecdotes*. 1963.

17. Harden, William. *Recollections of a Long and Satisfactory Life*. Savannah. Review Printing Company, Inc., 1928.

18. ———. *A History of Savannah and South Georgia*, Volume 1. Atlanta. Cherokee Publishing Company, 1981.

19. Jones, Charles C., Jr. *Sepulture of Major General Nathanael Greene and of Brig: Gen. Count Casimir Pulask*i.

20. ———. *The Life and Service of the Honorable Major General Samuel Elbert of Georgia*. Cambridge & New York. The Riverside Press, 1887.

21. Knight, Lucian Lamar. *Georgia's Landmarks, Memorials and Legends*. Atlanta, Georgia. The Byrd Printing Company, 1913.

22. McCall, Captain Hugh. *The History of Georgia*. Atlanta, Georgia. Reprint by A. B. Caldwell, Publisher, 1909.

23. *Marriages and Obituaries From Early Georgia Newspapers*. Abstracted by Judge Folks Huxford.

24. *Marriages and Deaths, 1820-1830, Abstracted from Extant Georgia Newspapers*. Mary Bondurant Warren with Sarah Fleming White. Danielsville, Georgia. Heritage Papers, 1972.

25. Newell, Cliff. *Savannah Now and Then*. Savannah, Georgia. The Printercraft Press, Inc., 1974.

26. O' Connell, Rev. Dr. J. J., O.S.B., *Catholicity in the Carolinas and Georgia: Leaves of Its History*. New York. D. & J. Sadlier & Co., 1820-1878.

27. *Register of Deaths in Savannah, Georgia, 1803-1853,* Volumes I-VI. Compiled by the Genealogical Committee of Georgia Historical Society. Savannah, Georgia, 1989.

28. Russell, Preston and Barbara Hines. *Savannah: A History of Her People Since 1733.* Savannah. Frederic C. Beil, Publisher, 1992.

29. *Savannah.* Compiled and written by the Savannah Unit, Federal Writers' Project in Georgia, Works Progress Administration. Savannah. Review Printing Company, 1937.

30. Shea, John Gilmary. *Life and Times of the Most Rev. John Carroll, Bishop and First Archbishop of Baltimore, Embracing the History of the Catholic Church in the United States 1763-1815.* New York. John G. Shea, 1888.

31. *Some Early Epitaphs in Georgia.* The Colonial Dames of Georgia, 1924.

32. Stokes, Thomas L. *The Savannah.* Athens. The University of Georgia Press, 1951.

33. *The Waring Papers: The Collected Works of Antonio J. Waring, Jr.* Edited by Stephen Williams. Cambridge and Athens. Peabody Museum of Harvard University and University of Georgia Press, 1965.

34. Vanstory, Burnette. *Georgia's Land of the Golden Isles.* Athens. The University of Georgia Press, 1956.

35. Wharton, Anne Hollingsworth. *Heirlooms in Miniatures.* Philadelphia and London. J. B. Lippincott Company, 1898.

36. Willsher, Betty and Hunter, Doreen. *Stones: A Guide to Some Remarkable Eighteenth Century Scottish Gravestones.* New York. Taplinger Publishing Company, Inc., 1979.

37. Wilson, Adelaide. *Historic and Picturesque Savannah.* Boston. The Boston Photogravure Company, 1889.

Papers, Pamphlets, and Documents

1. *An Ordinance for Enlarging the Cemetery or Public Burial Ground. Savannah, Georgia. July 29, 1789.* Georgia Historical Society Collection.

2. *Two Savannah Cemeteries* by Lillian Chaplin Bragg. *Georgia Magazine.*

3. Floyd, Dolores Boisfeuillet. *New Yamacraw and the Indian Mound Irene.*

4. Godley, Margaret and Bragg, Lillian. *Stories of Old Savannah.* Privately printed.

5. Heyward, Maude. *Illustrated Guide to Savannah, Georgia.* 1925.

6. Judge, Jane. *A Colonial Cemetery.* A paper found in the W.C. Hartridge Collection

7. LeMercier, Father Oliver. *A letter to the Right Reverend John Carroll, Bishop of Baltimore,* October 14, 1796.

8. McClenden, Robertine K. *Ambrose Gordon, 1751-1804: First of a Distinguished Family.* A paper. 1967. Courtesy of Juliette Gordon Low Birthplace.

9. *Panic in Savannah: The Yellow Fever Era.* A bulletin from Coastal Current Insight. Georgia Historical Society.

10. Russell, Preston. *Maitland (and Judge Lawrence) — We Are Here!* A paper. 1980. Courtesy of Dr. Russell.

11. Smith, Gordon B. *William Leigh Pierce.* A paper. From the Georgia Historical Society.

12. *The Burial Place of Button Gwinnett: A Report to the Mayor and Aldermen of the City of Savannah by the Savannah-Chatham County Historic Site and Monument Commission.* 1959.

13. *The Button Gwinnett Monument in Colonial Park Cemetery.*

14. *The Remains of Major-General Nathanael Greene.* A Report of the Joint Special Committee of the General Assembly of Rhode Island. Providence. E.L. Freeman & Sons, Printers to the State. 1903.

15. Thigpen, Thomas Paul. *Aristocracy of the Heart: Catholic Lay Leadership in Savannah.* 1820-1870.

Newspaper Articles

The Savannah Morning News

1. "Abercorn Street's Bones Cause Local Speculation" by Nancy Woods. May 4, 1967.

2. "Career of Women Who Aided Welfare of Savannah Told." November 30, 1950.

3. "Cemetery Move." April 22, 1972.

4. "Colonial Great Rest Here" by Chappie Atkinson. November 24, 1963.

5. "Dig Finds Bones Believed Maitland's" by Ron Wiginton.

6. "Epitaphs of a Century Ago" by Elfrida DeRenne Barrow. February 7, 1923.

7. "Gardeners Become Bricklayers To Restore Colonial Cemetery" by Cliff Sewell. September 20, 1970.

8. "Graves Mark Intriguing Era In City's Past" by Martha McArthur Shingler.   October 1, 1951.

9. "Lachlan McIntosh Chapter D.A.R. Celebrates 16th Anniversary: Sketch of General McIntosh" by Mrs. Ella Barrow Spaulding. February 18, 1917.

10. "Maitland's Bones to be Laid to Rest" by Ann Marshall Daniels. September 15, 1981.

11. "Malbone Portrait Given to Telfair." November 23, 1937.

12. "Miniatures by Malbone shown in National Gallery." April 21, 1929.

13. "Records Reveal Story of Slaying 100 Years Past" by Thomas Gamble. December 1, 1930.

14. "Savannah's Host to the Living and the Dead" by Thomas Gamble. March 22, 1925.

15. "Society of Colonial Dames Seeks to Preserve Cemetery." April 29, 1945

16. "The Battle For Savannah." July 7, 1997.

17. "The Story Behind Nathanel Greene Monument" by Shelby Myrick, Sr. November 23, 1958.

18. "To Exhibit Miniatures of Edward Greene Malbone" by Jane Judge. August 5, 1928.

19. "Two Medical Martyrs of Georgia in 1819-1820" by Victor H. Bassett, M.D. August 29, 1937.

20. "Two Women Doctors of Georgia in First Half of Nineteenth Century" by Victor H. Bassett, M.D. April 26, 1936.

21. "Vandals Wreck Old Tomb" photo by Ed Walsh. October 9, 1953.

22. " William G. Gaston Visits Savannah." April 12, 1925.

The Savannah Evening Press

1. "An Unrecognized Shrine" by Dan Nall. July 7, 1966.

2. "Bones Found at Cemetery's Edge" by Bert Emke. May 2, 1967.

3. "Colonial Cemetery: Burial Ground for Heroes" by Ralph Merkel. February 6, 1983.

4. "Historical Colonial Park: Treasured as a Tourist Shrine" by Kathy Palmer. September 28, 1963.

5. "Index to Graves in Colonial Cemetery." June 20 and 21, 1935.

6. "Police Probing Vandalism in City's Colonial Cemetery" by John Cramer. December 4, 1989.

7. "Savannah Vignette" by Beryl Sellers. July 7, 1966.

Savannah News-Press

"Lt. Col. John Maitland" by Ann Marshall Daniels. September 6, 1981.

Savannah Daily Times

1. "Some Quaint Epitaphs." April 17, 1887.

2. "Names of the Dead." November 13, 1854

The Georgia Gazette, 1797-1802.

The Republican and Savannah Evening Ledger, 1809-1819

Gazette of the State of Georgia, 1790-1792.

The Columbian Museum and Savannah Advertiser, 1802-1818.

The Atlanta Journal

"A Valiant Scot of Olden Georgia." April 18, 1926.

Collections

Gamble, Thomas. *Georgia Miscellany,* Volumes I-XI. A collection of news clippings and articles from numerous sources. Savannah-Chatham Public Library.

Hartridge, Walter Charlton. The Walter Charlton Hartridge Collection. A collection of many items of historical import pertaining to Savannah, including a photograph collection. Georgia Historical Society.

Matero, Frank. Colonial Cemetery Preservation Program Phase I. The Center for Preservation Research, Columbia University, NY. 1991.

MAP AND KEY TO COLONIAL CEMETERY

1. Anne Guerard
2. Gugel-Purse Vault
3. Theodora Ash
4. John Krieger
5. Edward Malbone
6. Wilson Graves
   a. Peyton & Mary M.
   b. Daniel Stewart
   c. Jane Dennis
7. Emily Thompson
8. Odrey Miller
9. Hugh McCall
10. James Cotton
11. Abbe Jean-Baptiste LeMoine
12. Gen. Lachlan McIntosh
13. Susannah Gray
14. Caroline DeRossignol Belleanse
15. Capt. Denis Cottineau
16. Legriel-DeIstria
17. Bridget Royston
18. Tucker, Ludlum & White
19. Three Unknown Skeletons
20. William Ray
21. Gabriel Leaver
22. Charles Rapp
23. John Evans
24. James Poince
25. Hannah Sheftall
26. Jacob Taylor
27. Josiah Muir
28. Richard J.S. Pinto

PERRY LANE

EAST WALL

ABERCORN STREET

53 Cahill

Sherlock

19 Skeletons

Unknown
54 Moore

Unknown
Brown

Unknown

17 Royston

18 Tucker, Ludlum & White

Unknown

20 Ray

Oliver

Sutcliffe
Thomasson

Foley
50 Malaurie
16 De Istria
Santini

21 Leaver
55 Hamilton
24 Poince
25 Sheftall

15 Cottineau
Halligan
14 Belleanse
13 Gray

22 Rapp
59 Lillibridge
23 Evans
26 Taylor

Unknown

12 McIntosh
Screven

McIntyre
Waldron
Unknown
Odingsell

40 Wilde
39 Cuyler
Christie
Johnston
Johnston

Flourney
Bevan

58 Masterton

White
10 Cotton
Burroughs

28 Pinto
27 Muir
56 Elon
Cleghorn
Unknown
Baldwin-Brigham
Unknown Wallace
29 Trowbridge
60 Struthers
30 Belcher

38 Gordon
Unknown
42 Woolhopter
41 Scarbrough

9 McCall 8 Miller
Millen
Unknown

11 LeMoine
Unknown

37 White
36 Gwinnett
Unknown

Schick
Thompson

7 Thompson
6 Wilson
5 Malbone
4 Krieger
Tebeau
3 Ash
Vincent

32 Waudin
34 Vickers
35 Bulloch
57 Elon
52 Mackay
51 McQueen
43 Morel
44 Williamson
Trevor-Hulse
2 Gugel-Purse

Tiot
47 Clay
Jones
31 Graham
Shellman
Lamb-Evans
Tufts
46 Cooper
45 Jaffrey

Davies
Unknown

Wylly
33 Habersham
Bolton
Hunter
1 Guerard

48 Elbert 49 Moravian Monument

D.A.R. GATES

OGLETHORPE AVENUE
(formerly South Broad Street)

29. Capt. Trowbridge
30. Grace Belcher
31. Graham-Mossman Vault
32. Joseph Waudin
33. Habersham Vault
34. Samuel Vickers
35. Archibald Bulloch
36. Button Gwinnett
37. Maj. Edward White
38. Elizabeth Gordon
39. Telemon Cuyler
40. James Wilde
41. Scarbrough Vault
42. Morecock-Woolhopter
43. Hannah Morel
44. William B. Williamson
45. William Jaffrey
46. Cooper Graves
     a. Capt. Jonathan
     b. Julia Ann
     c. Thomas M.
47. Joseph Clay
48. Samuel Elbert
49. Moravian Monument
50. Elizabeth Malaurie
51. John McQueen (Don Juan)
52. Robert Mackay
53. William Cahill
54. Sumner Moore
55. Alexander Hamilton
56. William Elon
57. Jane Elon
58. William Masterton
59. Hampton Baxter Lillibridge
60. John Struthers

ACKNOWLEDGMENTS

In any endeavor of this nature there are always individuals and groups who contribute a great deal to the success of a publication. They are invaluable to an author. The following provided me with technical advice, information, research materials, expertise, pictures, feedback and ideas. They are listed here with their contributions to this publication:

The Georgia Society of the Colonial Dames in America who first collected and published the epitaphs from Colonial Park in 1924.

Stacey Ann Yongue, Executive Director of the Scotland Arts Council of Laurinburg, NC, who spent many hours, visiting cemeteries with me, and taking photographs.

David Via, Cemetery Conservator, who provided me with much first hand information about gravestones, stonecutters, preservation, and techniques for reading worn inscriptions, and who always took time to listen and offer suggestions.

Stephen Bohlin-Davis, Curator of the Wayne-Gordon House in Savannah, who graciously took the time to read and edit the manuscript, and who provided me with old postcards and much information.

Don Gardner, Director of Savannah Park and Trees Department who described some of the burial vaults and offered other information as well.

St. Mary of Victory of the Cross, IHM; Georgia Spellman; and Rita Harper DeLorme of Savannah, who researched in the Catholic Archives for the information on Father LeMoine, Bishop John Carroll, and Father LeMercier, and who very graciously proofread this manuscript.

The late Monsignor Daniel J. Bourke of the Diocese of Savannah, who provided me with material from the Catholic archives.

Stephanie Jackel of Oglethorpe Press, who edited, offered suggestions, organized page layouts, guided me through the publishing process, and who published this book. Her patience was nothing short of phenomenal.

Preston Russell, who generously produced information on the removal of Col. Maitland's remains from the Graham-Mossman vault.

Dr. Michael Trinkley, Archaeologist with Chicora Foundation, Inc. who demonstrated the use of the penetrometer to locate unmarked gravesites, and allowed me to photograph him at work in Colonial Cemetery.

Carl Weeks, Savannah author and descendant of Peter Tondee, who provided me with information about his ancestor.

Lucinda Graham of the WD Photo Shop in Laurinburg, NC, who processed many rolls of film for me and made suggestions for some of the photographs.

Eric Wooddell of Savannah, GA, who offered me the use of his postcard collection.

Roger Smith, Director of the Massie School in Savannah, who searched out photographic information for me in the Massie archives.

Paul Blatner of Blatner's Antiques who provided me with the key to identifying the orientation of one of the old photographs.

Mary Beth D'Alonzo, Kimberly A. Ball, Jessica A. Burke, Mandi Johnson, and Frank Wheeler at the Georgia Historical Society, who spent many hours searching out materials that I requested, offered helpful suggestions, and photocopied materials.

Capt. Anthony A. Faust and Steffanie J. Baker of the Savannah Fire Department who provided information about the fire watchtowers and identified the tower in one of the photographs.

Sharen Lee, of the Thunderbolt Branch of the Chatham County Public Library, who introduced me to the Gamble Collection and often looked up reference information for me over the telephone.

A special thanks to Gene Carpenter, graphic designer, Savannah, for creating an accurate map from my amateurish attempts.

And to Jere Connan, of PressWorks, Savannah, who designed the cover of this book.

FULL NAME INDEX